Unwarranted Influence

Yale UNIVERSITY PRESS   NEW HAVEN & LONDON

Unwarranted Influence

Dwight D. Eisenhower
and the Military-
Industrial Complex

James Ledbetter

Yale University Press books may be purchased in quantity for educational, business, or
promotional use. For information, please e-mail sales.press@yale.edu (U.S. office) or
sales@yaleup.co.uk (U.K. office).

Set in Janson type by Integrated Publishing Solutions, Grand Rapids, Michigan.
Printed in the United States of America by Sheridan Books, Ann Arbor, Michigan.

Library of Congress Cataloging-in-Publication Data

Ledbetter, James.
Unwarranted Influence : Dwight D. Eisenhower and the military-industrial
complex / James Ledbetter.
p. cm. — (Icons of America)
Includes bibiographical references and index.
ISBN 978-0-300-15305-7 (hardcover : alk. paper)
1. Military-industrial complex—United States—History—20th century.
2. Civil-military relations—United States—History—20th century.
3. Eisenhower, Dwight D. (Dwight David), 1890–1969. I. Title.
HC110.D4L4 2011
355.02′130973—dc22   2010024512

A catalogue record for this book is available from the British Library.

This paper meets the requirements of ANSI/NISO Z39.48-1992
(Permanence of Paper).
10 9 8 7 6 5 4 3 2 1

ICONS OF AMERICA

Mark Crispin Miller, Series Editor

Icons of America is a series of short works written by leading scholars, critics, and writers, each of whom tells a new and innovative story about American history and culture through the lens of a single iconic individual, event, object, or cultural phenomenon.

Contents

Contents

Acknowledgments

The man who most made this book possible is Jonathan Brent, former editorial director at Yale University Press and now executive director and CEO of the YIVO Institute for Jewish Research. Over an engaging lunch, Jonathan not only grasped how this topic merited its own book but offered several penetrating insights that shaped how I approached my research and writing. His successor at Yale University Press, William Frucht, gave the manuscript a thoughtful and disciplined edit, banishing my more academic constructions. And production editor Jack Borrebach was indispensable in helping to organize the text and shepherd it to print.

Amy Tennery applied her dogged reporting skills to

helping with some of the research. Sara E. Berndt was able to provide a crucial document on a tight deadline. Mark Gimein was generous enough to read the draft manuscript and provide key criticisms and suggestions. Stephen Hess and Charles Griffin were gracious with their recollections and insights.

Of the many things I owe my literary agent Chris Calhoun, one of them is my deep gratitude for suggesting that I come up with ideas for Yale's Icons of America series. The entire project has been rewarding, from the initial brainstorming through the research and the final publication. The entire staff at the Eisenhower Presidential Library was friendly and helpful, but this book has especially benefited from the aid and scholarship of James W. Leyerzapf. I have also been ably aided by the staff at Columbia University's Oral History Research Office; by the Special Collections Staff at UCLA's Charles Young Library; and, most consistently, at the New York Public Library.

Most of all I thank my wife, Erinn Bucklan, whose enthusiasm and encouragement enrich my writing more than she can know.

ONE

Tracking the Unwarranted Influence

That Dwight David Eisenhower should be remembered for any speech at all—particularly one delivered late in his life—is something of a wonder. A world-renowned general, an Ivy League college president, an undefeated politician, and even a best-selling author, he was nonetheless not a great orator. Particularly after the 1955 heart attack and 1957 stroke he suffered, Eisenhower was known as a rambling, bumbling public speaker, especially when speaking without notes; in his press conference responses he often trailed off into half-sentences and non sequiturs. While some have suggested that he did so strategically, it is clear that much of his oratorical clumsiness was beyond his control. He once explained the effect of his stroke to an aide: "What happens is that the nerve in the brain that brings the right word to your mouth to express what you are thinking about doesn't work right, and sometimes a completely incorrect word shows up in your mouth."[1]

This is not to say that Eisenhower did not give significant, even great speeches. A few days before Election Day in 1952, he brilliantly encapsulated his authority on foreign policy and his predecessor's inaction with a simple, decisive (and cannily vague) statement: "I shall go to Korea." His sweeping "Chance for Peace" speech, delivered in 1953 in the wake of Joseph Stalin's death, had a dramatic worldwide impact. Even if, as many have maintained, its purpose was largely propagandistic, the text remains one of the seminal arguments against the expense and absurdity of a nuclear arms race. A somewhat related 1953 speech, often called "Atoms for Peace," is a rhetorical gem that has been closely examined for its multifaceted messages about Cold War strategy.[2]

Only one of Eisenhower's speeches, the one he gave just before he left the White House in 1961, has earned a permanent place in the public memory. Like any important address, it contained multiple messages and nuances, but its fame rests on a single sentence: "In the councils of government, we must guard against the acquisition of unwarranted influence, whether sought or unsought, by the military-industrial complex."

How has it happened that this rather dark sentence contains the most-cited words of a man who towered over American public life for some twenty years? This instance of historical concision—some might say elision—is remarkable for a variety of reasons. First, when thinking of memorable phrases from American presidents, the non-historian can rarely recall anything that presidents said upon leaving office. The most notable exception is Washington's farewell speech, which, as schoolchildren are taught, warned against permanent alliances. But most easily recalled presidential addresses draw their power from some other situation than departure. Lincoln's Gettysburg Address and FDR's "rendezvous with destiny" request for congressional action are memorable in large part as expressions of leadership during wartime. John F. Kennedy set the bar high for speeches of exhortation with his inaugural challenge to Americans to "ask not what your country can do for you—ask what you can do for your country." Books have been published about Jimmy Carter's "malaise" speech and Ronald Reagan's demand at the Brandenburg Gate: "Mr. Gorbachev, tear down this wall."[3]

There are good reasons why most memorable presidential speeches are not farewells, starting with the fact that there is no mandate for presidents to close out their time in office with a formal speech—and few do. Most two-term American presidents appear exhausted by the time they leave office, their relations with Congress and the press so frayed that their parting thoughts seem more likely to be torn apart than cherished in memory.

Second, depending on one's point of view, it is either ironic or contradictory or hypocritical that the man who first sounded a warning against a "military-industrial complex" was, by any definition, a leading figure in that complex. Not only because he spent almost all of his adult life in the American military and government—rising to the highest levels achievable in each—but because his eight years as president saw a dramatic buildup of nuclear weapons, which are among the stakes that make the influence of the military-industrial complex so frightful. The American nuclear stockpile grew from about 1,000 warheads in 1952 to approximately 23,000 by the time Eisenhower delivered his farewell speech. To many observers, this expansion suggests that the military-industrial complex had at least some influence on public policy while Eisenhower was president, raising the question of when, exactly, he decided it was something to watch out for.

Which leads to a third remarkable aspect of the message, and an apparent contradiction: it is well documented that Eisenhower himself did not coin the term "military-industrial complex." Indeed, none of the themes in Eisenhower's farewell address were directly generated by the president; they grew out of discussions among his speechwriting staff. Such separation of duties is typical in modern presidencies, and Eisenhower's aides have repeatedly insisted that he would never have delivered any significant speech unless he had reviewed and revised the text repeatedly and made the ideas his own. Nonetheless, there is some historical curiosity in the idea of a phrase, a moment, and a speaker becoming iconic while the actual authors remain obscure.

But of all the mysteries contained in the endurance of this sentence, the most tantalizing is that it is next to impossible to know what the president was actually talking about. In the half century since Eisenhower uttered his prophetic words, the concept of the military-industrial complex has become a rhetorical Rorschach blot—the meaning is in the eye of the beholder. The very utility of the phrase, the source of its mass appeal, comes at the cost of a precise, universally accepted definition. As historian Alex Roland succinctly put it in a 2007 essay, the military-industrial complex "was both a historical phenomenon and a political trope."[4] Tropes by definition constantly shift in meaning, and "military-industrial complex" (following a common convention, this book will deploy the abbreviation MIC) is as kaleidoscopically unstable as they come. Even Roland's use of the past tense implies a view of the MIC as historically complete that is far from universally shared. There is no military-industrial complex, but many military-industrial complexes—all of them defined by someone other than Dwight D. Eisenhower.

Summarizing from the variety of post-Eisenhower usages, however, we can approximately define MIC as a network of public and private forces that combine a profit motive with the planning and implementation of strategic policy. The overlap between private military contractors and the federal government is usually presumed to include, in addition to the military itself, areas of both the executive branch (Defense Department contracts and appointments of military contractors to government positions) and the legislative branch (lobbying by military contractors, campaign contributions, and the desire of members of Congress to protect and expand military spending that benefits their districts). Few argue that the MIC exercises any significant control over the judiciary, although it has been noted that judges are reluctant to rule against the federal government when it invokes national security.

It seems fair to say that the term "military-industrial

complex" is almost always used as a pejorative (even if its best-known usage was arguably neutral, in that Eisenhower warned not against the MIC itself but against its "unwarranted influence"). The case against the MIC is an indictment with multiple counts, to which any given critic may subscribe to varying degrees. These counts most prominently include:

The MIC creates wasteful military spending. This charge seems consistent with Eisenhower's concern, both in his farewell address and throughout much of his career. For decades, critics have charged that entire weapons systems have been kept alive at great expense, despite the absence of military need, largely or exclusively because they serve the interests of particular contractors or influential members of Congress. The B-1 bomber, for example, nicknamed "the born-again bomber," managed to enter production some thirty years after it was initially proposed, despite huge cost overruns, questionable military need, and inadequate performance. Even Jimmy Carter's decision to cancel the B-1 program in 1977 was not enough to put it away for good, leading some (not for the first time) to conclude that the MIC had grown more powerful than the president of the United States.

The MIC takes away from spending on social needs. This charge follows closely from the previous one: the MIC always finds ways to fund its needs, regardless of cost or necessity, while pressing American social problems such as poverty, illiteracy, infant mortality, and the shortage of affordable housing always seem to lack for money. Although this point of view was not explicit in Eisenhower's farewell address, it is consistent with his 1953 "Chance for Peace" speech.

The MIC distorts the American economy. This concern, too, follows directly from Eisenhower's parting speech: "We cannot mortgage the material assets of our grandchildren without risking the loss also of their political and spiritual heritage. We want democracy to survive for all generations to come, not to become the insolvent phantom of tomorrow." While Eisenhower focused specifically on military spending and the dangerous debt it could bring about, subsequent critics have raised much larger economic issues, arguing that the MIC distorts the value of the dollar, the volume and substance of U.S. trade, the types and locations of manufacturing jobs, and the markets for civilian applications of military technologies such as aircraft, satellites, and telecommunications.

Despite the obvious deviation that a military-industrial complex represents from the notion of a purely capitalistic economy, military spending and influence have rarely been a target for those who otherwise preach the virtues of free markets. At least since the Reagan era, American economic conservatives have by and large accepted that military spending—sometimes derided by others as "Pentagon capitalism"—trumps any ideological purity over the importance of free markets.[5] This makes the MIC a conspicuous anomaly; the postwar American political system has tolerated a commingling of private enterprise with the public purse in a military context far more willingly than in most other contexts (such as industrial policy, welfare, socialized medicine, or direct government funding of mass media—all relatively uncontroversial features of many Western democracies). Indeed, more far-reaching critics have described the MIC as a method by which vast amounts of wealth are transferred to the American economic elite more effectively and smoothly than could be done any other way.

The MIC has institutionalized an outsized role for the military in American society, even during peacetime. Before delivering his farewell address, Eisenhower and his advisors closely studied George Washington's farewell, which famously exhorted Americans "to steer clear of permanent alliances with any portion of the foreign world." In that speech, Washington less famously but no less urgently advised his countrymen to "avoid the necessity of those overgrown military establishments which, under any form

9

of government, are inauspicious to liberty, and which are to be regarded as particularly hostile to republican liberty." Although Eisenhower was a pragmatist who fully believed in America's modern role as a military superpower, he nonetheless was struck by how vast, pervasive, and permanent the American military had become since Washington's time, and he was deeply concerned about the implications. As America's involvement in the Vietnam War escalated, institutions such as the draft, military training on university campuses, and the long reach of military contractors into civilian life would cause many Americans to share his concern.

The MIC creates and extends a culture of secrecy. In focusing on science, technology, and university research, Eisenhower clearly intended to warn the nation that the MIC—even in his relatively modest formulation—could warp the very nature of intellectual inquiry by imposing strict secrecy requirements on fundamental research. In the late 1950s and 1960s, a ballooning portion of American university research was funded by the federal government, with military priorities usually taking the lead. To critics, this represented a colonization and corruption of institutions of learning, and a perversion of purpose for both individuals and communities who might well have taken a different path. As Derek Leebaert has written of

America's Cold War period: "'Secure' factories and labs, as well as millions of background investigations, did not come cheap. . . . Most knowledge is made to be shared; some is meant to be deeply private. The cult of secrecy all too often reverses the categories."[6]

The MIC leads to the suppression of individual liberty. For Eisenhower, this risk was grave but seemed mostly a concern for the future: "The potential for the disastrous rise of misplaced power exists and will persist. We must never let the weight of this combination [the military and industry] endanger our liberties or democratic processes." For subsequent critics, the MIC became the all-suppressing octopus, responsible for the denial of free speech, economic rights, academic freedom, the right to dissent, and even freedom of movement. Such charges have a stubborn longevity, stretching beyond the Cold War era and into the twenty-first century, as some argue that the fear of terrorism has become the new justification for the curtailing of freedom.

Given the extent of this indictment, it's not hard to see why critics of the MIC have wanted to invoke Eisenhower's authority, or why his presumed prophetic wisdom appears that much more admirable every time a critic finds another pernicious aspect of the MIC. It is precisely this historical elasticity that makes the term "military-industrial complex," the speech, and finally Eisenhower himself into icons.

Yet those who subscribe to this bill of particulars— whether or not they plausibly include Eisenhower as their ally—must confront a troubling question: If the MIC is such a bad influence, why has the United States failed to restrain it? While it would be an exaggeration to say that the MIC as defined has defenders, it certainly has beneficiaries and apologists.[7] Put another way, observers both inside and outside what could be called the MIC may accept the criticisms listed above yet still maintain that those negative outcomes are at least preferable to others. They point to the fact that the United States prevailed in its decades-long competition with the Soviet Union. Indeed, many have argued that one salutary effect of high levels of American military spending—regardless of how inefficient, or irrelevant to combat purposes—was to force the Soviet Union to match those levels, thereby breaking its economic back. In the post–Cold War environment— in which terrorism has usurped Communism as the overriding threat, and where the attacks of September 11 represented an incursion onto American soil on a scale that Communists never achieved—many of the same apologists argue that an MIC is still necessary to protect our citizens and way of life.

Those are the military parts of the apologia. On the industrial side, it is held that innovations that begin in military laboratories have beneficial effects on America's civilian economy. The Internet (which began life as ARPANET, at the Advanced Research Projects Agency of the Defense Department) and satellite communications are two well-known examples. Another argument is that military manufacturing is an important source of well-paying jobs in the United States, jobs that—because of their national security sensitivity—cannot easily be shipped abroad, even as globalization pulls the providers of so many other goods and services out of our borders.

This book will not pretend to adjudicate these debates. Its purposes are to describe the intellectual and historical origins of the *idea* of the MIC, to show how that idea has evolved in the wake of Eisenhower's speech, and to weigh contemporary arguments about the MIC using standards suggested by Eisenhower's views.

But the longevity of the concept of the MIC tells us something important about America's uneasy views about the intersection of arms, money, and political power. The specific forms that the MIC assumes today may not immediately resemble those from Eisenhower's experience as shaped by World War II and the early Cold War. He would probably not have predicted a protracted American military involvement in Iraq or Afghanistan, nor the commanding role that private contractors play in those conflicts; nor the use of torture and illegal wiretaps in the war against terrorism; nor the overwhelming American domination of the world's arms market. Yet to the extent that contemporary Americans struggle to square these difficult developments with democratic ideals, they use the remarkably durable frame of Eisenhower's speech from half a century ago. Even today, both defenders and opponents of the MIC seek to win the debate by pointing to the very terms Eisenhower articulated. Such a claim can be made by very few speeches, presidential or otherwise.

Thus, it is a mistake to speak of the MIC in the past tense. This book will demonstrate that the terms of Eisenhower's troubling critique have been used for decades to analyze the tension between democracy and military strength, and that today we still need to debate the concept of the MIC's "unwarranted influence" on the most fundamental functions of the American state.

TWO

Intellectual Origins

It is generally agreed—though not entirely true—that the phrase "military-industrial complex" did not publicly exist in the English language until President Eisenhower introduced it in January 1961.[1] Nonetheless, the phrase would not have resonated and endured as effectively as it did had it not synthesized several similar ideas that had taken wide hold in the first half of the twentieth century. Consider, for example, this passage from a book published in 1956:

> The decisions of a handful of corporations bear upon military and political as well as upon economic developments around the world. The decisions of the military establishment rest upon and grievously affect political

life as well as the very level of economic activity. The decisions made within the political domain determine economic activities and military programs. There is no longer, on the one hand, an economy, and on the other hand, a political order containing a military establishment unimportant to politics and to money-making. There is a political economy linked, in a thousand ways, with military institutions and decisions. On each side of the world-split running through central Europe and around the Asiatic rimlands, there is an ever-increasing interlocking of economic, military and political structures. If there is government intervention in the corporate economy, so is there corporate intervention in the governmental process. In the structural sense, this triangle of power is the source of the interlocking directorate that is most important for the historical structure of the present.[2]

Strip away the academic cadence, and this passage is practically a rough draft of the most famous section of the speech that Eisenhower would deliver five years later. Yet the author—the renegade sociologist C. Wright Mills, in his classic book *The Power Elite*—was politically and socially about as far from Eisenhower as possible (although both men had connections to at least one elite institution: Columbia University).

As improbable as it may appear on the surface, Eisenhower's invocation of the military-industrial complex tapped into widespread ideas about business, power, and the mil-

itary that had previously been espoused by outright paci-
fists or opponents of particular wars; by essayists and politicians (such as Woodrow Wilson) who favored the creation
of multinational organizations to prevent future wars; and
by sociologists concerned with the concentration of power
and the forms it was taking in twentieth-century societies.
The ideas of these critics can be placed into several categories.

- The merchants of death thesis. This theory,
  which became highly popular in the United States
  in the 1930s, holds that arms dealers cause, encourage, and perpetuate wars between nations so as to
  maximize their profits.
- The war economy thesis. This idea holds that too
  much of modern industry is tied to the production
  of weapons, and that the growing interdependence
  of the state and the arms industry is intrinsically
  dangerous. This argument, first advanced in
  Europe, took root in the United States and was
  developed into a full-blown economic theory by
  the 1940s.
- The garrison state thesis. This theory, which gained
  particular strength among academics during and
  after World War II, holds that large societies of
  the future would be organized in a highly military
  fashion, thus curtailing individual liberties and the
  ideals of democracy.
- The technocratic elite thesis. This notion holds
  that as American society becomes more complex

and more reliant on technology, it will be dominated by a class of unaccountable bureaucrats.

Examining each thesis in detail sheds light on the long-
standing political issues to which Eisenhower was alluding.

Merchants of Death

For nearly as long as a munitions industry has supplied
the U.S. military with weapons and supplies, there has
existed a worry that private companies would pursue
profit over duty to the national interest. Some historians
locate the origins of a military-industrial complex—and
the anxiety that it produced among some taxpayers and
legislators—as far back as the middle-to-late nineteenth
century.[3] There were, for example, accusations during the
Civil War that gun manufacturers provided substandard
equipment, often at outrageous prices. But the forging of
a permanent relationship between industry and the military began a couple of decades later. As the U.S. Navy
modernized its fleet in the decades after the Civil War, its
need for metal—first iron and later steel—expanded dramatically. Beginning in the 1880s, the U.S. government
began commissioning new steel cruisers, at the time the
largest peacetime expansion ever undertaken by the U.S.
military. The steel industry in this period was dominated

by a handful of companies, and the relationship between steel magnates, the shipbuilding industry, and the Navy became very close. For example, Benjamin F. Tracy, who was secretary of the Navy from 1889 to 1893 and an important proponent of constructing steel battleships, became an attorney for the Carnegie Steel Corporation upon leaving office.[4]

Along with government funding for the construction of railroads, funding for the new ships meant huge contracts for the steel industry. According to one congressional estimate, between 1887 and 1915 three steel companies—Bethlehem Steel, Carnegie Steel, and the smaller Midvale Steel—received $95.6 million in government contracts for a single product: armor plate for the Navy's ships.[5] The government was not buying a product that the steel companies were already making; there were no armor plate manufacturing facilities in the United States at the time. The government specifically subsidized the expansion of the steelmakers' capacity and granted patents for the manufacture of new products.

Perhaps inevitably, the flow of money and the competing interests of various parties created conflict. Accusations arose in Congress that a group of shipbuilders had received one million dollars in premiums because they'd built ships that could travel faster than the Navy had asked, with the suggestion that they colluded with government officials to get them. The House Naval Affairs Committee produced whistleblower evidence indicating that Carnegie Steel knowingly delivered shoddy armor plates to the Navy and had deceived government inspectors as to the quality of its product. In 1894, the chairman of the committee, Amos Cummings, charged that Carnegie employees "seem to have been somewhat animated by the desire to cheat the Government inspectors in every manner possible."[6] In its report, the committee concluded that "the frauds . . . found are worthy to be called crimes," which threaten "the dearest interests of the nation." A division of Carnegie eventually paid a fine of a little more than $140,000. Critics began to speak of an "armor ring" or, in the words of one Navy secretary, an "armor plate trust," thus applying the Progressive Era's lexicon of monopolies to the military contracting process.

Ever since then, charges of profiteering have regularly surfaced in the area of military procurement. Those charges took a qualitative leap around the time that World War I broke out. Not only would arms manufacturers cheat the government in order to preserve their profits, went the new argument, they deliberately encouraged countries to start wars, join wars, or prolong wars in order to create demand for their products. This was a more complicated and sinister charge, involving not only American companies but also arms dealers in Britain, France, and Germany.

While arms manufacturers formed patriotic leagues and "preparedness campaigns" with the goal of convincing America to enter the war, a handful of congressmen launched a far-reaching attack on munitions makers and suppliers of war materiel. The most tenacious was Clyde Howard Tavenner, an Illinois Democrat who served two terms in the House of Representatives beginning in 1913. His congressional career was relatively undistinguished, but in opposing World War I he had a powerful, if somewhat tainted, ally in Henry Ford. Tavenner explicitly accused the "war trust" not only of overcharging the government, but of driving the country to the brink of war. He cited both Washington and Lincoln as precedents for his view that military needs should be met through government-owned manufacturers, which was the only way to defeat the monopoly power of those who made weapons for profit. "Armor, armament and ammunition contractors are not big enough fools to cut each other's throats," he told Congress in 1915.[7] "Their business is to supply for a gigantic profit the wherewithal for the peoples of earth to enjoy a monopoly of throat cutting and tearing people limb from limb. As for themselves, they do not indulge in price-cutting warfare. Their game is purely profit making. They start the ball rolling by making nations distrustful of one another, and then in inducing them to overprepare for war. Does anyone doubt that if the European nations had not been so overprepared for war they would have been so willing to have entered into it?" The only solution to this path to war, he maintained, was to take the profit out of war and war preparation.

The rhetorical firepower of Tavenner and other opponents of World War I was ultimately no match for the interests who wanted America to join in, but the critique lived on. When the League of Nations was established in 1919, its Article 8 of statutes cited the "evil effects of private traffic in munitions," which was also the focus of a League conference in 1925. The merchants of death theory reached a kind of peak in the mid-1930s. The year 1934 saw the publication of three muckraking books: *Iron, Blood and Profits* by George Seldes; *Merchants of Death* by H. C. Engelbrecht and F. C. Hanighen; and a new edition of *War for Profits*, by Otto Lehmann-Russbueldt, translated from German. The books were notably similar; they were polemical histories of the arms industry going back as far as the Roman Empire. The principal indictments were that:

- Armament manufacturers operate outside the law, international treaties, or any system of accountability;
- They whip up war panics in order to secure a market and higher profit for their products;
- They directly cause some wars to happen, and prolong the duration of other wars;
- They justify their existence through appeals to patriotism, when in fact they undermine national security by selling materiel to their home country's enemies;
- They engage in bribery, bid-fixing, and other manipulative business practices that distort the free market.

These inflammatory charges—many of which were elaborations of Tavenner's work from a generation before—ignited popular outrage. Of the three volumes, *Merchants of Death* probably had the greatest impact. Advance orders caused its publisher to order a second printing even before the book's release on April 25, 1934, and a third printing the day after publication. It was the Book of the Month Club's lead selection in May 1934, and indeed the Seldes book was "rushed through the press" in order to compete with it.[8] *Merchants of Death* became a best seller and was translated into French, Dutch, and Spanish.

The timing of the books coincided with the most sustained and critical American legislative interrogation of the arms industry, which became known as the "munitions inquiry," led by Senator Gerald P. Nye of North Dakota. In April 1934, the Senate passed a resolution—without a dissenting vote—asserting that "the influence of the commercial motive is an inevitable factor in considerations involving the maintenance of the national defense," and indeed that it is "one of the inevitable factors often believed to stimulate and sustain wars." When Nye began his hearings—with a staff that featured a recent Harvard Law School graduate named Alger Hiss—in September 1934, he was poised like few before or since to fundamentally alter the way in which America arms itself. He had, at least officially, the support of President Roosevelt to conduct a far-reaching inquiry, and he began to take seriously the notion that the U.S. government ought to have absolute control over the production of war materiel, a position supported by a majority of Americans according to opinion polls of the time.[9] "There is certainty that the profits of preparation for war and the profits of war itself constitute the most serious challenge to the peace of the world. . . . The removal of the element of profit from war would materially remove the danger of more war," Nye said in November 1934.

This was the political high-water mark for the forces of

disarmament and isolationism in American life. During this same period, Senator Arthur Vandenberg of Michigan had introduced a resolution advocating taking the profits out of war—which was supported by the pacifist Women's International League, as well as by the American Legion—and Congress also seriously considered making neutrality the official legal position of the United States. Yet despite holding numerous hearings and eliciting many embarrassing details about the arms trade, the Nye committee never accomplished much more than issuing reports filled with salacious charges but few viable alternatives. Nye charged that powerful interests were conducting "a large effort to slow up the investigation," which was probably true; committee hearings about arms shipments abroad caused much diplomatic flurry. But there were other problems. Nye and Roosevelt had never gotten along well, and Nye felt that a separate committee appointed by the president to examine the profits of war was designed to undermine his own. Noting that the president's committee was loaded with military personnel, Nye bitterly compared it to appointing John Dillinger to write the anti-crime laws.

But most important from a public opinion point of view, Nye stepped on some crucial historical toes. In January 1936, Nye and another senator on the committee, Bennett

Champ Clark of Missouri, put into evidence documents indicating that Woodrow Wilson and his secretary of state had, in the spring of 1917, falsely stated that they had no knowledge of secret treaties tying Great Britain to various plans to carve up Europe upon an armistice to end World War I. Going outside the scope of the committee's mandate was bad enough, but to call Woodrow Wilson a liar was simply too much. The following day, Senator Tom Connally from Texas rose, as one historian puts it, "to give Nye one of the most scathing tongue-lashings ever administered on the Senate floor."[10] Connally thundered: "Some checker-playing, beer-drinking, back room of some low house is the only place fit for the kind of language which the Senator from North Dakota . . . puts into the Record about a dead man, a great man, a good man, and a man who when alive had the courage to meet his enemies face to face and eye to eye." Connally pounded his desk so hard that a knuckle on his left hand became permanently misshapen. The following day, Senator Carter Glass of Virginia, who had served in Wilson's cabinet, called the attack on Wilson "not only destitute of decency but . . . a shocking exhibition as never has happened in the 35 years I have served in the Congress." Glass, too, exhibited his anger physically; his fist-slamming caused his hand to bleed. This was the end of Nye's ability to conduct an effective inquiry, and the merchants of death thesis—at least in Washington's power centers—went into hibernation for decades.

The War Economy Thesis

The war economy thesis is a close corollary of the merchants of death thesis; both involve the intersection of commercial activity and the military. But the war economy thesis reaches further: it holds that modern industrial states are so intertwined with the manufacturers of military equipment that they are mutually dependent. An important claim of the war economy thesis is that modern warfare—with its incorporation of aircraft, and its voracious appetite for industrial products using steel, rubber, and petroleum—intrinsically and inexorably reduces or eliminates the distinction between a society's civilian and military needs.

World War I was undoubtedly the crucible for this line of thought. As the war began in 1914, a group of liberal and radical intellectuals and journalists in Great Britain formed an influential antiwar organization called the Union of Democratic Control (UDC). Among the better-known figures in and around the UDC were Bertrand Russell and Charles Trevelyan. The UDC published numerous pamphlets attacking Britain's role in the war; they held public rallies attended by thousands throughout the country; and they played a crucial role in making the Labour Party, rather than the declining Liberal Party, the dominant force of the British left in the early twentieth century.[11] Their critique of the Great War and Britain's role in it had many facets, including condemnation of Britain's history of "secret diplomacy" (by which diplomats made promises to support other nations in wars, without approval from Parliament or the public) and the role played by the international arms trade.

However, some in the UDC developed a broader criticism of the unprecedented symbiotic relationship between the military and civilian economies. In a strictly military sense, this thesis had been brewing since the nineteenth-century idea of "total war," after the development of steam power, the magazine rifle, smokeless gunpowder, and other modern military technologies.[12] The UDC extended the idea of total war into every facet of a modern country's economy. In a remarkably prescient book published in 1914, the left-wing journalist Henry Noel Brailsford, who served on the UDC's governing board, wrote: "The events of the past two years have shown that modern warfare will henceforth be waged with increased implacability, not against the armies and navies of the contending Powers alone, but against the civilian population, which by its monetary contributions, by its manufacture of the fuel of slaughter, by its agricultural and industrial labours, and by its sanction, maintain those armies and navies. It will be impossible for belligerent States, and more and more futile for international lawyers, to draw any distinction between combatants and non-combatants. It is flying in the face of logic to maintain that the man (or woman) who fashions the projectiles or the explosives which another man discharges, with deadly effect, is a non-combatant."[13]

World War I provided ample evidence to adherents of the war economy theory on both sides of the Atlantic, and indeed there was a strong mutual influence between the UDC's beliefs and Woodrow Wilson's arguments, beginning in 1916, for a peace settlement and the establishment of a league of nations.[14] The U.S. entrance into the conflict in 1917 may have shattered that affinity, but for proponents of the war economy thesis, that move simply corroborated their beliefs. Although charges that the United States entered World War I for largely economic, as opposed to military or strategic, reasons were highly controversial in the 1930s and helped derail the Nye committee's work, subsequent historians have accepted this view with little fuss. Wilson's desire to keep America neutral in the Great War is well known, and the country was ill-prepared militarily to intervene against a German nation that had been arming itself for decades, but the fact remains that the United States faced keen economic pressure to violate its desired neutrality. As early as the summer of 1914, large American banks began pressuring the Wilson administration, through Secretary of State William Jennings Bryan, to allow them to make substantial loans to the French government and to the powerful Rothschild family, which controlled much of the French banking system. Officially, Wilson and Bryan were opposed to such moves; Bryan declared that "money is the worst of all contrabands," and he wrote to the head of J. P. Morgan that "loans made by American bankers to any foreign nation which is at war are inconsistent with the true spirit of neutrality" (although this statement is something less than an outright prohibition).

Unofficially, however, the tug of the Great War on the American economy proved impossible to ignore. In October 1914, an official at the National City Bank contacted the State Department and noted that American manufacturers were asking to issue credits to foreign buyers of U.S. wares, in order to take advantage of the "unprecedented and increasing volume of goods." If American companies did not provide such credits, the banker noted, Europe's belligerent powers would simply turn elsewhere—Argentina, Australia, Canada—thereby rendering U.S. neutrality not only pointless, but harmful to its own economic interest. Wilson agreed, thus launching the U.S. financial system on a dangerously slippery slope of its own design. Credits became loans; banks became overly dependent on the loans; the belligerent powers could not repay the loans, which thereby threatened the banks. Within a few years, the Wilson administration found itself facing a potential meltdown of the world financial system. As one Wilson biographer put it, the president had to "deal, therefore, with commercial impulses that were as great a threat to neutrality as the emotions of moralists."[15] Just as the efforts of total war required an all-out mobilization of a country's economy, so, too, did a fully functioning economy seem to require trading with the warring countries—or even joining them.

This book is not a venue to adjudicate the historical debate about precisely why the United States entered into World War I (although it is worth noting that Wilson himself testified before the Senate Foreign Relations Committee that he believed America would have entered the war even absent any German action against U.S. citizens). But whatever guided the U.S. course of action, historians and public figures of the time had established the notion that modern industrial economies act interdependently with modern military institutions for ill effect. The idea is closely akin to what Eisenhower would several decades later call "unwarranted influence, whether sought or unsought, by the military-industrial complex." Of the four concepts discussed in this chapter, the war economy thesis is the only one that had actual policy proponents, as opposed to apologists, enablers, or self-interested advocates. Even before World War II came to an end, influential businessmen and policymakers argued that the United States needed to place its industrial capacity on a more permanent war footing. In January 1944, Charles Wilson, the former president of General Motors and the executive vice president of the War Production Board, delivered a landmark speech before the Army Ordnance Association. He denounced previous strategies of disarmament as "thoroughly discredited" and asserted that the nation's security depended on maintaining the ability to go to war at any moment. He looked to the longstanding concept of maintaining a naval fleet "in being"—that is, not to engage an opponent but to deter war by drawing an opponent's forces to defend against possible attack. "What is more natural and logical than that we should henceforth mount our national policy upon the solid fact of an industrial capacity for war, and a research capacity for war that is also 'in being'? It seems to me that anything less is foolhardy." He called for the armed services and private businesses to work in tandem to harness science and technology for military preparedness, and for industry to be allowed to play its role unhampered "by political witchhunts, or thrown to the fanatical isolationist fringe tagged with a 'merchants-of-death' label."[16] Wilson would later become secretary of defense in the Eisenhower administration.

No doubt many of the businessmen who made up Wilson's audience were delighted at the prospect of continued government money flowing their way even during peacetime. On top of that, the government also knew that war spending was good for the economy and began to sense that it could be beneficially extended to peacetime as well. The 1930s and 1940s saw the birth of a school of thought that would become known, somewhat misleadingly, as "military Keynesianism": that a government's military expenditures are a legitimate way to stimulate (or, depending on the proponent, sustain) economic growth. Through most of American history, war taxes and war expenditures were generally only enacted according to temporary military need, but the shape of the global economy at the end of World War II prompted high-ranking U.S. policymakers to consider the benefits of a permanent war economy. As early as January 1944, Secretary of State Cordell Hull began considering a massive postwar strategic hoarding program, in which the United States would stockpile over a period of five years materials—crude rubber, industrial diamonds, tin, petroleum—that it would conceivably need in a future war. In addition to the obvious benefits for military preparedness, importing the materials would have a positive economic side effect. As a *Wall Street Journal* account from the time put it, the plan "would provide a balance for the large-scale American export program that is in prospect for world reconstruction, offering a way for debtor nations to repay public loans advanced by this country."[17]

In broader economic terms, the mobilization for World War II had achieved something very close to full employment in the United States. Maintaining it was a desirable enough social goal that Congress gave the federal government responsibility for promoting "maximum employment, production, and purchasing power" in the Employment Act of 1946. At the time, military-related expenditures represented approximately three-quarters of all government spending, and so simply complying with the mandate of the Employment Act, at least in the near term, meant heavy reliance on military expenses. Many in the government would accept that situation as economic pragmatism. But on the American left, the notion of a permanent war economy was attacked because its expenditures would be intrinsically unproductive—building tanks and fighter planes does little to satisfy human needs—and because it would concentrate power in the hands of monopoly capitalists. It was also seen as a cynical jobs-building gimmick. The editors of the left-wing magazine *Politics* wrote: "In war, modern capitalism has . . . an economic stabilizer better than pyramids, cathedrals and WPA rolled into one."[18]

There is a curious, little-known episode from this era that is germane to the present discussion. It is rare, in discussions of popular criticism of military spending from the period between the wars, to glimpse how these debates were viewed inside the military itself. In the summer of 1930, *The Nation* magazine published a brief but unusual exposé entitled "The Profits of War." In it, a law professor named Forrest Reserve Black claimed to have seen internal War Department memoranda from 1924 indicating that for several years the government had been contracting with private manufacturers to supply materiel for a yet-to-be-declared war. According to Black, an agreement called the War Department Adjustable Price Contract guaranteed munitions makers a certain level of production and a price that would include a "normal" profit; the contract would come into effect upon declaration of war or similar national emergency. Citing an almost certainly pseudonymous military source named "Major Mars," Black asserted that the War Department was acting "upon the advice of big business men and of the National Association of Manufacturers."[19] Black noted that there was no specific legal authority for such a provision, and he predicted that munitions makers would exploit war hysteria in order to extract the highest possible price from the government. "If the American people really desire to prevent a repetition of 1917–18 they ought to demand full information about this War Department alliance with business interests; for experience has proved over and over the dangers to peace that lurk in the profits of war," Black wrote.

The article caught the eye of the editor of the *Manitowoc Times* in Wisconsin, who wrote an editorial accusing the War Department of "an outrageous assumption of power." This, in turn, caught the eye of the office of the assistant secretary of war, which felt the need to set both publications straight. A letter was drafted for General George Van Horn Moseley to sign, politely pointing out to each publication that there was indeed a congressional authorization for such mobilization, the National Defense Act of 1920. Furthermore, the general asserted that there was a public interest in rationalizing the military contracting process that had gone awry during World War I. The drafting, editing, and mailing of the letters was overseen by an assistant within the War Department: Dwight D. Eisenhower.[20]

The Garrison State Thesis

There are certain phrases that carry especially strong resonance for a time. In the 1940s and 1950s in America, it was common for public officials to caution against becoming a "garrison state." The precise meaning of the phrase depended on the user; at times it was used to describe what would later be called a "satellite state" or a "buffer zone" in a military context, a territory of citizens whose fate was largely determined by the needs of a larger, more dominant power. More frequently—and it's not hard to see the evolution between the connotations— it was used to describe a society in which individual liberties are severely constricted and automatically subservient to state and military imperatives. In 1947, for example, a *New York Times* writer summarized the dilemma of the nuclear age this way: "In seeking security we must be careful that we do not lose freedom. For there can be a trend—given the threat of the atomic bomb—to increase military power in all fields more and more to such a degree that the ultimate end would be the 'garrison state.'"[21]

The most thorough formulation of the idea came from the sociologist Harold Lasswell, who published an essay in 1941 entitled "The Garrison State."[22] In Lasswell's view, the garrison state was distinguished as "a world in which the specialists on violence are the most powerful group in society." The modern supremacy of the businessman's skills of negotiation and profit would, in a garrison state, give way to the supremacy of a soldier's skills of fighting and technical mastery. Of particular note was the role of the military in maintaining public order. Lasswell focused specifically on the development of aerial warfare as a factor that abolished the distinctions between civilian and military interests. He imagined a population that would be compelled to work, for the supposed good of the state, while most democratic institutions would disappear in favor of dictatorial decision making and government by plebiscite. Economic production would be regularized, and the rulers would use "war scares" to ensure that the population did not overconsume. Not surprisingly, Lasswell imagined that "those standing at the top of the military pyramid will doubtless occupy high positions in the income pyramid."

Lasswell presented the garrison state as a "developmental construct," a scenario in many ways increasingly likely to come about, but one that could be avoided with proper study and assertion of democratic values. For an American academic writing in the midst of the Second World War, he was remarkably objective about where he expected the garrison state to arise: he identified Japan, Germany, Russia, and the United States as strong possibilities. Were such a state to come about in the United States, he predicted, it would be organized—ironically enough—around the "symbol pattern" of a unified democracy among free states. That is, the United States and certain allies would conspire to destroy freedom in order to save it.

Lasswell was not some lone academic wolf. In a somewhat shocking 1950 address, Claude A. Putnam, head of the National Association of Manufacturers, declared matter-of-factly that Americans were "going to live in a garrison state for five, ten or fifteen years."[23] It is a bleak vision, but millions of Americans glimpsed some version of it, if only as a goal to protect against. Of course, most Americans believed that their Constitution and democratic heritage were a bulwark against what was also beginning to be widely labeled as "totalitarianism." But that view was severely challenged by the rise of antidemocratic regimes abroad; by domestic constrictions on liberty during World War II (the internment of tens of thousands of Japanese Americans particularly disturbed many); and by the fact that much of the globe even after the Allied victory was beginning to resemble a garrison state.

One American who expressed the fear of a garrison state and his aim to oppose it was Dwight Eisenhower; the phrase is sprinkled throughout Eisenhower's private and public communications. In a press conference not long after becoming president, for example, Eisenhower described the difficulty of assessing and meeting the threats to the United States: "We don't want to become a garrison state. We want to remain free. Our plans and programs have to conform to a free people, which means essentially a free economy. That is the problem that, frankly, this Administration meets on, discusses, works on every day of its life."[24]

In a radio address a few days later, Eisenhower explicitly made a connection between military spending, the illusion of total security, and the specter of dictatorship: "It is fact that there is no such thing as maximum military security, short of total mobilization of all our national resources. Such security would compel us to imitate the methods of the dictator. It would compel us to put every able-bodied man in uniform—to regiment the worker, the farmer, the business man—to allocate materials and to control prices and wages—in short, to devote our whole nation to the grim purposes of the garrison state. This—I firmly believe—is not the way to defend America."[25]

These quotations do not suggest that Eisenhower was specifically referring to Lasswell; Marxist-tinged sociology was not Eisenhower's preferred reading material. Nor can simply substituting "military-industrial complex" for "garrison state" fully describe Eisenhower's meanings in either instance. Still, the record is clear—and we shall see other examples in later chapters—that Eisenhower believed from the very early days of his presidency that if America was to live up to its mission, strict lines had to be drawn between national security and military spending on the one hand, and liberty—particularly economic liberty—on the other.[26]

Fear of the Technocratic Elite

The 1940s and 1950s saw dramatic technological developments throughout American society. The atomic bomb and, later, the hydrogen bomb were viewed not only as military developments but as the culmination of scientific progress that many feared had spun out of control. Television and the computer brought great benefits to American life, but they also challenged the ways that many lived their lives. Indeed, a substantial portion of Eisenhower's farewell speech warned against the antidemocratic possibilities inherent in misuse of scientific and technological knowledge.

This theme was a common undercurrent in postwar thinking. In its extremes, the fear of a technocratic elite took the form of dystopian fantasies, such as George Orwell's novel *1984*. But less extreme versions also dominated 1950s thinking. The fear was that even the institutions that we love and admire could conspire to progressively rob us of our individuality and our values. Among the most popular books of the mid-1950s were Sloan Wilson's *The Man in the Grey Flannel Suit*—a novel about the soulless life within the American corporation, adapted as a popular film starring Gregory Peck—and William H. White's *The Organization Man*, a book about the domination of personality by big business.

A related fear existed of the perhaps-too-persuasive powers of television and advertising. Intellectuals worried that public opinion research could be refined to the point where individuals could be monitored and even manipulated. Advertising executives spoke openly of applying mass psychological techniques to the public, creating consumer behavior that exploited human needs without necessarily satisfying them. Eisenhower's chief speechwriter in the second term, Malcolm Moos, worried about the application of such methods to the political process. "Increasingly public-relations and advertising men have figured in political campaigns. And this is a circumstance that provokes many misgivings. The importance of the advertising or public-relations man to the party cannot be underestimated, for these professionals have become expert in the use of mass media," Moos wrote in a book published in 1956.[27]

The fullest expression of an American elite and the consequences for American democracy came from the sociologist C. Wright Mills. His 1956 book *The Power Elite* systematically catalogued the centers of power concentrated in a few sectors of society: notably, business, the military, and national government. Mills's concern was that a schism had appeared in American society, between an elite with ever-increasing control and a mass society with little to no identification with, or leverage upon, the elite. Needless to say, this was a destructive development in a democracy, and Mills was among the decade's most caustic and pessimistic critics of how elites were manipulating civic discourse in modern America: "Public relations and the official secret, the trivializing campaign and the terrible fact clumsily accomplished, are replacing the reasoned debate of political ideas in the privately incorporated economy, the military ascendancy and the political vacuum of modern America."[28]

As with Lasswell and the garrison state, there is no suggestion that Eisenhower himself ever read Mills (although Moos certainly did). Yet there are passages of *The Power Elite* that are so thematically close to Eisenhower's farewell speech that it almost seems surprising that Mills did not himself coin the phrase "military-industrial complex." Having begun this chapter with a passage from Mills that seemed to anticipate Eisenhower, let us conclude it with a passage from Eisenhower that seems to echo Mills:

> Today, the solitary inventor, tinkering in his shop, has been overshadowed by task forces of scientists in laboratories and testing fields. In the same fashion, the free university, historically the fountainhead of free ideas and scientific discovery, has experienced a revolution in the conduct of research. Partly because of the huge costs involved, a government contract becomes virtually a substitute for intellectual curiosity. For every old blackboard there are now hundreds of new electronic computers. The prospect of domination of the nation's scholars by Federal employment, project allocations, and the power of money is ever present—and is gravely to be regarded. Yet, in holding scientific research and discovery in respect, as we should, we must also be alert to the equal and opposite danger that public policy could itself become the captive of a scientific-technological elite.

THREE

War, Peace, and Eisenhower

It is one of the great ironies of Dwight Eisenhower's life that he was the son of pacifist Mennonites. His parents, David and Ida Eisenhower, were members of the Brethren in Christ, a pacifist sect established during the eighteenth century in Pennsylvania Dutch country, where the Eisenhower ancestors settled in the 1740s. Dwight, who was born in Abilene, Kansas, in 1890, was raised with his brothers in a home that prohibited alcohol, smoking, card playing, and swearing. War, too, was considered a sin. Ida was a self-taught biblical scholar who, in Stephen Ambrose's words, "grew up listening to numerous stories about the horrors of the [American Civil] war, which reinforced the pacifism that went with her religion."[1]

When, as a child, Dwight began to show a voracious appetite for military history—to the extent of neglecting chores and schoolwork—his mother was disturbed and tried to keep the family's history books locked in a closet.

It would be sophomoric to suggest that Eisenhower's upbringing left him with a deep-seated antipathy toward war. But more than many in the armed forces, he brought to his military career an intellectually and psychologically nuanced view of warfare. When he moved into the White House, his ideas about war and the proper role of the military would often conflict with the views of others, and his beliefs could be themselves contradictory.

Accidental Soldier

Eisenhower's undistinguished early military career offered little promise of what he would later achieve. After graduating in the middle of his West Point class in 1915, he was stationed in San Antonio and recruited to coach the football team at a military academy. To his dismay, he never saw combat during the relatively brief U.S. involvement in World War I, and he was frustrated by an Army bureaucracy that seemed to value only his administrative abilities. During a tour of duty in Panama beginning in 1922, he began to develop relationships with fellow soldiers, such as Fox Conner and George Patton, that would later prove valuable. In the early 1920s, he completed a course at the War College and then was sent to Europe for fifteen months to assemble a guide to battlefield monuments of the Great War. (The assignment pleased his wife, Mamie, who vastly preferred Paris to Panama.)

Toward the end of 1929, Major Eisenhower—he would retain that rank for a surprising sixteen years—was given one of the meatiest assignments of his career between the wars. As part of his duties within the Department of War, he was called upon to produce a series of reports on "industrial mobilization": that is, how the American economy could be adapted for maximum military effectiveness in wartime. The following year, Congress created the War Policies Commission to study the relationship between profiteering and war, with an eye toward a possible constitutional amendment that would prohibit private companies from making a profit from munitions and allow the government to seize private property in the event of war. Eisenhower spent much of 1930 and 1931 planning industrial mobilization for war and providing the commission with necessary information from the War Department.

Eisenhower's biographers tend to skim over this episode, except to note that it was the first time he worked directly with the Army's new chief of staff, Douglas MacArthur.[2] And granted, even though the commission hearings were prominent in Washington in 1931, little became of them; the work, as Stephen Ambrose wrote, "went on in a vacuum."[3] Yet the assignment placed Eisenhower at the center of the politics of war profiteering. The commission was created to placate the increasingly strident voices of World War I veterans and the American Legion, who were demanding universal conscription as a way of redistributing the burden of war, as well as excess profit taxes on military contractors or outright nationalization.[4]

Eisenhower was enthusiastic about the assignment, which took him all across the country and into Mexico, and with his typical mastery of detail he immersed himself in the most minute aspects of the industries that supplied war materiel. He included not merely those with obvious connections to combat, such as tank and gun manufacturers, but also more general businesses, notably rubber producers. The U.S. military had a vast appetite for rubber—for tires, tank tracks, seals, gaskets, piping, shock absorbers—and was concerned that its supply, most of which came from the East Indies, could be cut off in wartime by a naval blockade. By 1930, Eisenhower was remarkably expert in all aspects of rubber production, and he prepared a lengthy paper on how to secure alternative supplies if peacetime rubber sources were dramatically reduced. Even two decades later, this experience seemed to shape his view of how world trade should work. When he went to Paris to organize the NATO alliance in 1950, a friend lamented that while the future president recognized the need for a system of free trade, it was almost entirely because he "seemed preoccupied with the military importance of U.S. access to tungsten and other strategic materials."[5] As John Lewis Gaddis observed, once Eisenhower entered the White House, "press conference questions [on trade] regularly elicited presidential lectures on the critical importance of foreign manganese, cobalt, tin, and tungsten, in terms both worthy of and gratifying to future New Left critics of American capitalism."[6]

The questions posed by industrial mobilization were much larger and more complex than the rubber business. Just as the critics of war economy recognized the interdependence of a society's military and its economy, so did the military. A 1930 article for the journal *Army Ordnance*, written by Eisenhower for his superior, Assistant Secretary of War Frederick Payne, asserted that "today a nation faced with a grave military emergency must look as anxiously to her capacity to forge the weapons of war as she does to the ability of her Army and Navy."[7] In a historical paper on procurement and mobilization prepared for the Army Industrial College, Eisenhower noted that a plan for wartime industrial mobilization, "to be of any value, must be a joint Army-Navy-Business Man's plan."[8]

So in wartime, industrial mobilization seemed critical. But what, exactly, would mobilization consist of? Would the presidents of large companies take on high military rank and be forced to produce according to military orders? Would it entail the creation of "super-agencies," akin to the War Industries Board during World War I, with the power to procure war materiel separate from the War Department? This was not what the military in the 1930s wanted. Rather, it sought a series of "gentlemen's agreements" under which individual businesses accepted that, in an emergency, they would have to devote up to 50 percent of their productive capacity for military needs, and where necessary create "government corporations" for sensitive areas such as marine insurance, shipbuilding, and power.

Another key provision of industrial mobilization was price controls. Eisenhower and his colleagues in the assistant secretary of war's office understood that increased military demand for products (particularly imports such as rubber, tin, nickel, iodine, and manganese) would lead to shortages. Shortages in turn could lead to price hikes, and, as Major Eisenhower put it, "when prices begin to rise in war they rush in dizzy spirals to heights that cannot fail to have the most demoralizing influence on the whole population."[9] Naturally, the federal government would have to control production and pricing, since no other entity would have sufficient authority. In addition, the mobilization plan called for the country to be divided up into "fourteen procurement districts," each with a chief who would carry out orders from the president and the War Department.[10] Effectively, the plan had the commander in chief sitting atop the nation's supply chain.

For Eisenhower, this was a harsh, precarious way to organize an economy, justified only by the emergency of declared war. Having such strictures in place during peacetime could violate constitutional protections and the principles of the free market. The importance of keeping a peacetime separation between business and the military would stay with him for the rest of his life.

"We Are Going to Damage the Country Financially"

Eisenhower's position in World War II as supreme commander of Allied forces was unprecedented. Never had one man had such far-reaching authority over all branches of the military; never had such authority been exercised successfully on an intercontinental scale. From that heady perch Eisenhower naturally developed an unrivaled perspective on military organization, effectiveness, and efficiency. Congressional overseers of military affairs, generals and admirals, even White House staff—none could match the mastery Eisenhower brought to questions of national security, organization, military budgets, and strategy.

Yet Eisenhower's experience of war and its institutions also gave him an idiosyncratic, often controversial set of views on how the armed forces are paid for, deployed, and maintained. In addition, air power, atomic weaponry, and the dramatic emergence of the Cold War fundamentally changed nearly every assumption about America's military and its place in the world. Whether anyone agreed with Eisenhower or not, he brought to the table a commander's authority on military matters that was only enhanced once he became president—and he did so in an environment where the old prewar verities did not necessarily apply.

Eisenhower's opinions about warfare and the military—which were born as soon as he reached West Point but only blossomed at the end of World War II—are worth exploring in some detail. Take, for instance, nuclear weapons. Eisenhower did not initially agree with many of his colleagues in the military and government that the atomic bomb was an effective way to end the war with Japan.

At the Potsdam Conference in 1945, as the former Allies and Axis powers divided up postwar Europe, the conversation among many principals turned to the development of the bomb. Eisenhower learned of its existence from Secretary of War Henry Stimson, who had overseen the Manhattan Project. "I expressed the hope that we would never have to use such a thing against any enemy because I disliked seeing the United States take the lead in introducing into war something as horrible and destructive as this new weapon was described to be," Eisenhower recalled a few years later. "Moreover, I mistakenly had some faint hope that if we never used the weapon in war other nations might remain ignorant of the fact that the problem of nuclear fission had been solved. I did not then know, of course, that an army of scientists had been engaged in the production of the weapon and that secrecy in this vital matter could not have been maintained."[11] Once he occupied the White House, his view would be tempered, but the instinctive reaction is telling: Eisenhower looked at weapons not in a narrow tactical sense but in terms of how they affected the overall balance of power.

A recurring theme of Eisenhower's writing, before and after he was elected to the White House, was the need for a rational military policy that balanced the duties, budgets, and roles of the Army, Navy, and Air Force. His experience as Allied commander in World War II led him to believe that future American wars would require coordination among the three, but it had also taught him that infighting, politics, and special pleading in the branches were a constant waste of time, money, and energy. In a 1945 letter to his hometown friend and lifelong correspondent "Swede" Hazlett, the future president made the case that both taxpayers and the civilian government needed to get a proper overall picture of military needs and expenditures if they were to make the right policy decisions. "Since war is a triphibious matter, how can you make any judgment upon this matter at all—whether you are in private life or whether you are chairman of a Congressional Committee—*unless the broad yearly program for all three Services is presented to you as a unit?* Do you not need to know whether ground forces have been provided to complement the navy and air, and the navy both the others? If the members of each of these Services—and remember that service pride and esprit in each are equally strong—come to you *unilaterally* and plead for support, I am unable to see how you can get a balanced picture."[12]

The question of military expenses and the overall public good came up again, in another letter to Swede in 1949. Eisenhower—by then president of Columbia University, a position he held from 1948 to 1953—was frustrated by the seeming inability to discuss whether weapon systems were worth the money without being accused of being antimilitary. "The current task of getting every one to approach these questions from the single viewpoint of the country's good—and without unreasonable prejudice or bias in favor of some particular theory or weapon is truly difficult," he wrote. "I am quite certain that unless we rapidly arrive at some sensible solution of this problem we are going to damage the country financially and without adding to its defensive strength."[13] He continued: "The subject is no longer discussed, in Washington, in terms other than those of controversy. If someone expresses doubt as to the great effectiveness of the B-36, then he is instantly 'anti-Air'; if someone else sees weakness in the theory of employing a supercarrier or mildly objects to the Navy's developing a land Army, in time of war, of 600,000 Marines (which it did in World War II), then he is called 'anti-Navy.' All this distresses me greatly."

At this time, Eisenhower began to formulate economic principles that had been underplayed in his earlier writings but were nonetheless consistent with his background and future viability within the Republican Party. (He had been a supporter of Roosevelt and was courted by the Democratic Party, but as a solid pro-business midwesterner, he would not have been comfortable as a Democrat in the 1950s or any subsequent decade.)

While he was president of Columbia, Eisenhower delivered a sweeping philosophical defense of private enterprise against many of the criticisms made by socialists and
Communists. "Our system is based upon the concept that
each person is an individual, with dignity and certain in-
alienable rights," he told a group of twelve hundred sales-
men at a lunch at New York's Roosevelt Hotel in 1948. "It
has been said that we uphold property rights in the free
enterprise system against human rights. I say that is a
false statement. The right to property is only one of the
human rights, and when that falls all else falls with it. The
abolition of property rights means an eventual dictatorship. We have been criticized for our large numbers of
unemployed during the early Nineteen Thirties. That was
held up as a condemnation of the capitalistic system. But
those men were not working in the salt mines, and they
were not under the whip and bayonet. You business men
can prove to the world that a free democracy can, and
shall, continue to exist on this continent."[14]

If this was political boilerplate, designed to shore up
Eisenhower's credentials for a presidential run, it was also
a heartfelt declaration of Eisenhower's view of economic
liberty. Intriguingly, the second speaker at the luncheon
was W. Walter Williams, a prominent Republican banker
from Washington State, who warned of the economic

threats that could arise from imprudent military spending as the nation prepared for the Cold War: "We must arm effectively, but this program has serious implications in our economy. No one knows what the cost of rearmament will be, but some have estimated it at $30 billion. What effect will that have on our tax structure? Will we be faced with deficit financing? There is also the question of what will happen to our freedom if we live in a garrison state." To what degree Eisenhower agreed with these sentiments is a matter of conjecture, but after Eisenhower became president in 1953, he appointed Williams undersecretary of commerce.

Balance and the Budget

It is a truism, bordering on a cliché, to say that Eisenhower always sought a balance in his approach to public policy. Even so, it is worthwhile to frame his two terms as president in terms of some very important balances, the first of which is the balance between spending on national security and fiscal responsibility.

When he took office, Eisenhower confronted a situation that few modern presidents have faced: the wholesale demilitarization of the American economy. When World War II ended, the American economy was on a total war footing. The financial sector was completely caught up in the funding of war; the industrial sector was completely engaged in producing the materials for war; and large percentages of the workforce were employed either in war-focused manufacturing or in the military itself.

Even if the Truman administration had made demilitarization of the economy its highest priority, it would have been a multiyear task, and once the Korean War began, there was little possibility of doing so. Truman's last three years in office saw the military budget increase from a little more than $13 billion in 1950 to more than $50 billion in 1953. This led to a near doubling of the federal budget, one of the most rapid rises in the modern history of federal spending.[15] When Eisenhower took office, his budget director broke down federal spending into three categories: national security; major programs that were nearly impossible to cut, such as debt service, price supports, and veterans' benefits; and everything else. The first category accounted for nearly two-thirds of all federal spending.

The extent of the government's debt obligations was not widely appreciated in Congress. Considerable pressure for tax cuts came from within Eisenhower's own party. Republicans had not held executive power for two decades and were anxious to return the country to fiscal priorities and a vision of limited government that had been abandoned during the New Deal and World War II. But given the continuing expenses of the Korean War, tax cuts were bound to worsen deficits. The outgoing Truman administration had run deficits of more than $13 billion in its budgets for 1952 and 1953, and it estimated the fiscal 1954 deficit would be $10 billion. Eisenhower's advisors were convinced that the situation was actually far worse; they had found unfinanced authorizations for spending—primarily on rearmaments stemming from the Korean War—going back to 1950, amounting to a staggering $81 billion of debt.[16]

Eisenhower was a lifelong believer in balancing the budget and minimizing the federal government's control over the economy. If progress toward these goals was to be made, military appropriations would have to be cut. His early budgets slashed government expenditures against howling congressional opposition. The wind-down of the Korean War in 1953 made defense budget cuts possible—hundreds of thousands of men were decommissioned from the military—but it also had a dampening effect on the economy, which went into recession in the middle of that year. Unemployment reached 6 percent in January 1954.

There was a fundamental tension within Eisenhower's administration between those who shared the president's goal of a balanced budget and those who believed that no expense should be spared in the military contest with the Soviets and their allies. The balanced-budget camp included Director of the Budget Joseph Dodge and Treasury Secretary George Humphrey; the military camp included Secretary of State John Foster Dulles and Defense Secretary Charles E. Wilson (who, as we saw, was an early architect of the idea of a war-based economy).[17] From the first days of his administration, Eisenhower insisted on re-evaluating all "basic national security policies and programs in relation to their costs." Toward this end, he added the treasury secretary and budget director to the National Security Council.

Wilson, nicknamed "Engine Charlie" to distinguish him from "Electric" Charlie Wilson, the former CEO of General Electric, was an outspoken member of the cabinet who made unwanted waves. A journalist noted in mid-1953 that his "bull-in-the-china-shop behavior continues to distress the White House staff."[18] In a contentious meeting that fall, he drew his line in the sand: "If we ever go to the American people and tell them that we are putting a balanced budget ahead of national defense, it would be a terrible day." Yet that is more or less what the administration chose to do, even if it never publicly framed its choice so starkly. The president believed that if

America simply spent money in any place and on anything claimed to be militarily necessary, it would bankrupt its economy and/or destroy its liberties, crushing the very freedoms its spending was intended to uphold. John Lewis Gaddis has referred to the need for restrained military spending to *preserve* American economic liberty as "probably the most persistent single theme of Eisenhower's public and private utterances while in the White House."[19]

The New Look

The administration's approach to national security policy, frequently tagged the New Look, was intended to promote fiscally sound military strength, support for non-Communist allies abroad, and competition with Communists where they were attempting to exert influence. The principles of the New Look were codified in a secret document called NSC 162/2, approved by the administration in October 1953.[20] Today most historians consider the New Look a mixed success; the growth of nuclear weapons and rising challenges to American power in the Middle East and Latin America muddied the administration's purpose. But a crucial aspect of the New Look, and a significant shift from the previous administration's nuclear policy, was that it contemplated the retaliatory use of nuclear weapons even in conflicts that began with conventional weapons. Experts called this "asymmetric response." Secretary of State Dulles gave a handier summary in a 1954 speech, arguing for the ability "to massively retaliate" against Communist aggression.[21]

Although the New Look had some strategic rationale, the major factor behind its introduction was economic. One of the chief goals of NSC 162/2 was "to avoid seriously weakening the U.S. economy or undermining our fundamental values and institutions."[22] Shifting the American promise of security to the threat of massive nuclear retaliation was a way to save money, since nuclear warfare would not require the same troop strength as reliance on ground or naval war. Accordingly, the administration's fiscal 1955 budget cut $5 billion in defense spending from the previous year, as some 500,000 troops were taken out of the Army. (There was therefore a relative strengthening of the Air Force, the service that presumably would launch a nuclear attack on the Soviet Union; its share of the defense budget rose to nearly half in the mid-1950s.) These reductions had bitter opponents in Congress— particularly Stuart Symington, the Democratic senator from Missouri who had also been secretary of the Air Force—and in the military. In congressional testimony in 1953, Air Force Chief of Staff Hoyt Vandenberg declared:

"The numerous and somewhat contradictory administrative and fiscal actions of the past few months have caused the greatest amount of uncertainty and confusion in the Air Force and among allied activities that has existed since the demobilization after World War II."[23]

And so the New Look, while apparently a plausible response to the nation's growing indebtedness and the increased Soviet threat, had the support of neither the complete cabinet, nor key congressional leaders, nor many of the military top brass. Moreover, by committing the United States to a long-term reliance on nuclear weapons, the New Look strategy had the effect of accelerating an arms race with the Soviets that, as H. W. Brands puts it, "rendered the United States more, not less, threatened."[24]

The impact of relying on nuclear weapons, however, was far greater than simply economic or military. New Look policies committed the United States to prolonged cooperation with NATO and other allies abroad; to covert operations against the Soviet threat, real or perceived; and to active U.S. involvement in even minor disputes across the globe, lest they be exploited by the Soviets or other enemies. But perhaps the most important effect was the realignment of public opinion. Beginning in the summer of 1953, the administration undertook a top-secret effort, initially known as Project Candor, designed to in-form the American public about the full implications of living in the "Age of Peril."[25] Its far-reaching efforts included a series of presidential speeches warning the public about the extent of the threat and the prolonged nature of conflict with the Soviets, a television series, an Advertising Council campaign, and a public awareness program about the need for blood drives and even bomb shelters.

On one level, such a propaganda campaign made sense: for a nuclear threat to be effective, it must be both plausible and terrifying. At the same time, its psychological effects belied the very notion of "security." Eisenhower explicitly agreed to consider the use of nuclear weapons in any scenario where U.S. interests might justify it—in a 1955 press conference, he said that "I see no reason why they shouldn't be used just exactly as you would use a bullet or anything else."[26] The administration effectively scared the daylights out of not only the American people but also allies and potential allies, who could envision atomic bombs being dropped on their soil if it were unlucky enough to become the locus of U.S.-Soviet aggression. These were not abstract or empty threats; even before the official adoption of NSC 162/2, Eisenhower had obtained limited Chinese cooperation to end the Korean War by dropping hints to India about American willingness to use atomic weapons, knowing the Indians would pass this on to the Chinese and Soviets.[27] Many historians have judged the Eisenhower administration rather harshly on this score, some referring to a policy of "apocalypse management" or the construction of a "national insecurity state."[28] The policy of deliberately frightening the American population could not easily be contained, and when opponents of Eisenhower's administration harnessed that fear to complain that too little was being done to match alleged Soviet military might, the administration was hoist with its own nuclear petard.

Chance For Peace

Much of the administration's nuclear policy was surely inevitable. Eisenhower was the first president whose time in office was completely framed by the Cold War, and while tensions between the United States and the Soviet Union preceded Eisenhower's presidency, his was the first White House that had to grapple with the very real prospect that the Soviet Union would match or even exceed America's nuclear arsenal. The Soviet detonation of a hydrogen bomb in August 1953 would have galvanized any White House occupant. As a result, the debate within the Eisenhower White House was not whether to embrace nuclear weapons but whether and how to contain their costs. Given the other strategic options on the table at the time—such as actively attempting to "roll back" Soviet control of Eastern Europe, or committing land troops to fight Communist China—the New Look was hardly the most confrontational.

More important, Eisenhower was not only a fearmonger. A significant second balance to grasp is that as president, Eisenhower tried to promote diplomatic openings to the Soviets and their allies. When he took office in early 1953, the long-term chill in U.S.-Soviet relations was not a given. The death of Joseph Stalin in March 1953 created tremendous uncertainty within the U.S. government as to who was actually in charge of that country; within that uncertainty there lived a degree of hope for a thawing of relations or even forms of cooperation between the two nations. The Soviets fueled that hope with a short-lived peace initiative; Soviet leader Georgi Malenkov began speaking of "peaceful coexistence" and proposed an East-West summit.

Eisenhower and his advisors saw an opportunity, and also saw that it might be brief. Thus was born an extraordinary presidential address on the issues of freedom, peace, and economics: the "Chance for Peace" speech, delivered on April 16, 1953, in Washington, DC, before the American Society of Newspaper Editors. The speech—Eisenhower's first major address as president—was carefully crafted and much labored over, not only by White House staff but also by senior figures in the State Department, including Secretary of State Dulles and outgoing official Paul Nitze. It was designed as a major address with substantial foreign policy implications, an olive branch offered to the Soviets with near certainty that it would be rejected, but intended to score propaganda points worldwide. For this reason, there were significant internal debates about the timing of the speech; the effect it would have on negotiations about the fledgling European community; the effect it would have on Korean armistice negotiations; and how much emphasis should be placed on achieving goals like the liberation of Eastern Europe before agreeing to negotiate more broadly with the Soviets. The level of preparation, debate, and secrecy that went into "Chance for Peace" was such that in addition to specific textual recommendations on a draft, Nitze wrote a four-page, single-spaced memorandum about general goals and considerations for the speech. He had consulted with various European diplomats and United Nations officials, and his memo remained classified as top secret for nearly thirty years.[29]

The "Chance for Peace" speech, in what had become fairly standard Cold War rhetoric, offered a stark vision of a world divided into a sector that respected freedom and a sector that didn't. Still, what is most remarkable is not the finger-pointing at the Soviets but the president's comments on how wasteful and exhausting a protracted Cold War would be (even as his administration was preparing for precisely that). If there was no change in the hardening of transatlantic relations and no move toward freedom in Soviet-controlled areas, Eisenhower said, then these were the worst-case and best-case scenarios: "The worst is atomic war. The best would be this: a life of perpetual fear and tension; a burden of arms draining the wealth and the labor of all peoples; a wasting of strength that defies the American system or the Soviet system or any system to achieve true abundance and happiness for the peoples of this earth."[30]

The president argued not merely that war was destructive and undesirable, but also that spending on war, even during peacetime, diverts resources that could be put to better use.

> Every gun that is made, every warship launched, every rocket fired signifies, in the final sense, a theft from those who hunger and are not fed, those who are cold and are not clothed. This world in arms is not spending money alone. It is spending the sweat of its laborers, the genius of its scientists, the hopes of its children.
>
> The cost of one modern heavy bomber is this: a modern brick school in more than 30 cities. It is two

electric power plants, each serving a town of 60,000
population. It is two fine, fully equipped hospitals. It
is some fifty miles of concrete pavement.
We pay for a single fighter plane with a half million
bushels of wheat.
We pay for a single destroyer with new homes that
could have housed more than 8,000 people.
This is, I repeat, the best way of life to be found on
the road the world has been taking. This is not a way
of life at all, in any true sense. Under the cloud of
threatening war, it is humanity hanging from a cross
of iron.

As Blanche Wiesen Cook has shown, the "Chance for
Peace" speech had a massive impact across the globe.
It was recorded, translated, published as a pamphlet, and
pushed out through every government propaganda organ.
The U.S.-funded radio stations in Eastern Europe pumped
out hourly summaries of the speech on the day it was delivered; in India, more than a hundred thousand handbills
were distributed in eight languages.[31] Never before, and
rarely afterward, did a U.S. president so passionately and
prominently lay out a vision for ending tensions with the
Soviet Union or so frankly criticize the social costs of
military spending.

Such sweeping rhetoric, straying so far from the normal presidential posture regarding the American military,
raises a nagging question: Did he mean it? It is impossible

to ignore the fact that, despite the widespread praise lavished on the speech, the administration did next to nothing to follow it up. Granted, within months the shakeout in Soviet leadership produced a confrontational leader, Nikita Khrushchev, who in many ways was just as implacable as Stalin. But even where unilateral American action might have made a difference—such as channeling savings from disarmament into a fund for world aid and reconstruction—the speech's ideals did not become an administration priority. The post-Stalin thaw never happened.

John Emmet Hughes, who worked closely with Eisenhower on the speech, questioned whether the president's heart was really in it. "Throughout its delivery, he had looked ashen and ill, for he had painfully suffered from food poisoning since the night before. And as so much time passed without giving sign of reverting to the spirit or promise of that occasion, the wry thought occurred that he almost acted as if the event itself had left some unpleasant aftertaste."[32] That might be the bitter recollection of a former aide, but there was a common perception that the administration was not eager to return to the themes of "Chance for Peace." Coming back from a trip through the western states, Henry Cabot Lodge, the administration's ambassador to the United Nations, told the White House staff: "I heard everywhere one major criticism—that promises of action on the foreign field don't seem to have been kept. There's just a widespread feeling of no follow-up to the sweeping declarations of last April." John Lewis Gaddis and Tom Wicker have both concluded that despite his lofty rhetoric, Eisenhower was unwilling to genuinely engage the Soviets in 1953 because he feared giving any of the post-Stalin leaders too much authority; he preferred to let them squabble amongst themselves.

This is the type of paradox that often confronts Eisenhower biographers and that seldom can be satisfactorily resolved. The president's apparent ambivalence regarding atomic weapons, however, may have a simple explanation: nuclear weapons were too new, too terrifying, and too disruptive for anyone in 1953 to know what the United States should do with them. The "Chance for Peace" speech is the best-known piece among much evidence that Eisenhower genuinely believed that nuclear nations might agree to place these weapons off-limits and effectively turn them over to international control agencies. In what reads like an exasperated moment on the last day of 1953, Eisenhower implied that the United States might actually be better off without such weapons at all, writing to C. D. Jackson: "I should like to discuss with all the so-called 'military experts' just what would be the effect on us and our position if atomic weapons could be wholly eliminated from the world's armaments. . . . We must consider the factor that atomic weapons strongly favor the side that attacks aggressively and *by surprise.* This the United States will never do; and let me point out that we never had any of this hysterical fear of *any nation* until atomic weapons appeared on the scene and we knew that others had solved the secret."[33] Nuclear disarmament may have been an unrealistic wish, but it tantalized Eisenhower throughout his presidency.

A Peace Movement Is Born

While genuine disarmament might have never gotten a serious hearing inside the Eisenhower White House, it was nonetheless a popular topic. Immediately after the United States unleashed two atomic bombs in 1945, millions of Americans—many of them well known, including many nuclear physicists—struggled to think of ways in which such weapons could be formally barred from future deployment. Many of the early antinuclear activists were advocates of world government.[34] Like activists in the disarmament movement of the 1920s and 1930s, they found sympathy and support among elected officials and other prominent public figures.

In June 1949, for example, eight thousand people gathered in Madison Square Garden to support a resolution, introduced by Democratic senator Glen Taylor of Idaho, advocating that the State Department make it a specific goal of American foreign policy that the United Nations be developed into a world federation. (Taylor had been the vice-presidential candidate on Henry Wallace's Progressive Party presidential ticket the year before.) The chief speaker that evening, Supreme Court justice William O. Douglas, spoke of the need for a world government in terms similar to Eisenhower's argument in "Chance for Peace" a little less than four years later. Douglas acknowledged that the movement for world government, especially if backed by the United States, could be rejected by the Soviets, but he insisted that it was a desirable goal nonetheless. "Even then, the Western World can assuredly find in world government new hope and promise for peace. Even then we can have a new instrument of government, not merely a defensive pact. Even then we can unite to manage jointly many of the central problems of peace."[35] He was followed by Cord Meyer, Jr. (later a significant official in the CIA) and Senator Charles W. Tobey of New Hampshire, who had joined with twenty-one others to sponsor the resolution in the Senate. A similar resolution had ninety sponsors in the House of Representatives. Referenda supporting such goals had passed in both Connecticut and Massachusetts, and more than half of state legislatures had urged Congress to act.

Even as the administration committed itself to increased reliance on nuclear weapons—and the secrecy, testing, expense, and radioactive fallout these weapons entailed—to ward off the Soviet threat, a growing group of American citizens began to see nuclear weapons themselves as the threat. Not only did these weapons force the United States into a permanent war footing, according to the activists, they rendered meaningless the very concept of national sovereignty. Albert Einstein was the informal leader of this group, but its chief polemicist was Norman Cousins, probably the most energetic and activist editor of his era. No editor of comparable prominence combined Cousins's breadth of interest, the depth and commitment of his humanism, and his remarkable access to the most powerful men in the world.

Cousins's vehicle was the *Saturday Review*, a tiny, struggling literary magazine that was a spinoff supplement of the then-liberal *New York Post*. The *Review* had some offices in the same building as *Current History*, a magazine established at the outbreak of World War I to provide American readers with a perspective on global affairs, where Cousins was hired in the 1930s after a stint as the

Post's education editor. There he befriended Henry Seidel Canby, a Yale professor and literary critic who founded the *Review*. Canby liked Cousins's energy and intellectual acuity and added him to the *Saturday Review* editorial staff in 1940, making him editor in 1942 at the tender age of twenty-seven.

Cousins took to his task with a fearless zeal, spurred on by the urgency of World War II. He did not fight in the war but worked as a consultant to the Office of War Information. Cousins felt that the best way for America to influence affairs outside its borders was to spread its art, literature, and culture abroad, as well as practical know-how about building housing and infrastructure. With the dropping of the atomic bomb on Hiroshima in August 1945, he believed, mankind had entered a new, frightening era. In the first of many crusades during his long editorship, Cousins published a passionate *Review* editorial entitled "Modern Man is Obsolete," in which he maintained that the understanding of war that had existed for centuries was no longer viable. In an era of atomic weapons, no nation could go to war with another nation to protect its national security without risking its own—and the world's—annihilation. War was no longer something that could be won; indeed, "man's survival on earth is now absolutely dependent on his ability to avoid a new war."

From this, Cousins concluded that "the greatest obsolescence of all in the Atomic Age is national sovereignty." The sole path on which mankind could move forward was toward cooperation among nations and collective decision making, while rejecting the legacy of nuclear weapons. "There is one way and only one way to achieve effective control of destructive atomic energy, and that is through centralized world government." The editorial, published as a slim book, became a national bestseller.[36]

For Cousins, these concerns could never be confined to the pages of a magazine; they were causes to fight in the world. He became a consultant to General Douglas MacArthur during the postwar occupation of Japan and was especially struck by the aftereffects of the bomb, whose use, MacArthur told him, had been militarily unnecessary.[37] After visiting Hiroshima in 1949, Cousins devoted himself to helping women in the city who had been disfigured by the bomb. He photographed women with horrendous burns—women who often refused to be seen in public or would wear masks—brought the pictures to plastic surgeons in the United States (particularly at Mount Sinai Hospital), and persuaded them to operate on the women for free. With help from Kiyoshi Tanimoto, a Methodist minister featured prominently in John Hersey's book *Hiroshima*, more than 140 women—dubbed the

"Hiroshima Maidens"—were flown to the United States for such treatment beginning in 1955. Readers of the *Saturday Review* were also encouraged to adopt Japanese infants orphaned by the bomb; Cousins and his wife themselves adopted a daughter. Today, a monument to Cousins stands in the Peace Memorial Park in Hiroshima.

Cousins saw no conflict between humanist activism, his magazine work, and participation in practical politics. He was a close friend and advisor to Adlai Stevenson, the Democrat whom Eisenhower defeated in the 1952 and 1956 presidential elections. And thanks in part to a cross-country speaking tour that Cousins took in the early 1950s, he had a good sense for what Americans were thinking and feeling. The formula worked well; under Cousins's impassioned editorship, the *Saturday Review* became one of the most influential magazines in postwar America, with a circulation that would eventually grow to 600,000.

In the politically polarized era of the early twenty-first century, the idea of a meaningful connection between a leftist advocate of nuclear disarmament and a Republican military president might seem preposterous. Perhaps it seemed so then, too. The early 1950s were, after all, the height of McCarthyism, and Cousins had to deal with charges that he was a Communist dupe. This isn't to imply that Cousins had the same influence on Eisenhower as the president's golf buddies; they rarely met in person during Eisenhower's presidency, and while Eisenhower did invite Cousins to write a speech for him in 1959, the speech was never given.[38] Moreover, Cousins and his activism were occasional thorns in the administration's side. The Eisenhower State Department was highly concerned about the public relations impact of even as innocuous a project as the Hiroshima Maidens.[39] Cousins and Eisenhower would eventually disagree publicly about a moratorium on nuclear testing.

Yet throughout the 1950s the two men maintained a serious and respectful, if occasionally contentious, correspondence. The record strongly suggests that through his persistence, diplomacy, and moral reasoning, Cousins functioned as a kind of nuclear conscience for the president, the representative of a set of principles that would become increasingly important as Eisenhower aged. As the "Chance for Peace" speech demonstrates, Eisenhower's own views could sometimes be powerful tools, at least rhetorically, for those advocating disarmament.

FOUR

Eisenhower's Contentious Second Term

Despite his health problems, Eisenhower's re-election in 1956 was a foregone conclusion, and he ended up winning forty-one states and nearly 58 percent of the popular vote. Yet the political ease of the election did not last. The last years of his presidency were marked by deep, often bitter conflicts with Congress over the military and national security. These conflicts represented, to some degree, genuine differences of opinion about spending levels and policy direction, but within the administration it was widely perceived that congressional Democrats and their allies in the military and intelligence communities were inflating and distorting military issues for political gain. This rankled Eisenhower, who tended to believe that no one—including the chiefs of staff—had a better understanding than he did of the needs and limitations of the American military.

These conflicts came to a head in the fall of 1957, with the one-two punch of the Soviet Sputnik launch and the near-simultaneous release of a report arguing that the United States would soon fall behind the Soviets in the production of atomic weapons. The president's frustration at these developments led him—and many around him—to believe that the military had become an interest group unto itself rather than a mere instrument of policy, and to seek approaches to national security outside the traditional military.

Yet even before the Sputnik launch, Eisenhower appeared to be shifting away from the view that nuclear weapons were a cost-effective method of achieving security with few side effects. His meditations about the moral, military, and scientific complexities of nuclear weapons were often prompted by his correspondence with Norman Cousins. In the summer of 1956, Cousins published a sweeping *Saturday Review* editorial entitled "Think of a Man." Returning to the themes he had outlined in his post-Hiroshima editorial, he briskly summarized the entire intellectual history of mankind—from art and literature to medicine, science, and architecture—and argued that for the first time in human history, it could all be wiped out. "There is no achievement in human experience, no record, no thing of beauty that cannot now be rescinded and all its benefits and traces swept into void," he wrote. "Earlier generations have had the power merely to affect history; ours is the power to expunge it."[1] He then touched on the questions of nuclear testing, radioactive fallout, and the need for a wholesale re-evaluation of the idea of security in a world that he believed had moved beyond the sovereign state.

As usual, Cousins tried to maximize the impact of his cri de coeur. Believing he was addressing the most important issue facing mankind, he engaged in unabashed self-promotion, sending copies of the editorial far and wide. Advance copies went to the presidents of major universities, several prominent clergymen, the entire Senate Foreign Relations Committee, various officials of the United Nations, the Supreme Court, the board of directors of the Advertising Council, and prominent men such as John D. Rockefeller and Oscar Hammerstein—and of course his occasional correspondent Dwight D. Eisenhower.

It would be entirely reasonable to think that a sitting president three months from re-election would simply ignore such an idealistic missive or have his staff issue a perfunctory response, especially if the editorialist was identified with the president's opponent and publicly opposed his views about national sovereignty and the need for a nuclear test ban. (The test ban issue was important in the 1956 presidential election, with Adlai Stevenson in favor and Eisenhower opposed.) Yet something in Cousins's argument rekindled the vision Eisenhower had expressed in his 1953 "Chance for Peace" speech.

Eisenhower replied to Cousins on August 6—the eleventh anniversary of the bombing of Hiroshima—to say he found the editorial "powerful and persuasive." He had had similar thoughts, he wrote, upon learning of the first explosion of an atomic weapon and of plans to drop one on Japan, and "never has the matter ceased troubling me." He touched on the apparent difficulty of getting modern Americans to focus on the difficult issues of disarmament and individual action: "It seems to be an historical fact that when a people become strong, prosperous and on the whole contented with their lot, it becomes very difficult to reach them with an idea that requires them to think of unpleasant possibilities or to undertake the work and effort required to eliminate such possibilities."[2] The letter was not all praise; Eisenhower reminded Cousins of the technical difficulty of monitoring nuclear weapons built by a country intent on concealing them. But he also promised to circulate the article among close associates.

Politicians, of course, often write to constituents to assure them their ideas are receiving the utmost consideration. Yet there is ample reason to believe that in the summer of 1956, Eisenhower was indeed contemplating Cousins's disarmament position. In his memoir, Eisenhower advisor and chief speechwriter Arthur Larson wrote: "In one of our sessions in August 1956, he asked me if I read the *Saturday Review*. I said yes, and expressed the opinion that it was becoming an important periodical on public affairs, especially through its editorials. At that point he handed me a copy of Norman Cousins's editorial on the hydrogen bomb which had made a deep impression on him."[3]

Eisenhower clearly had an appreciation for Cousins's writing. Malcolm Charles Moos, the speechwriter hired in late 1957 who would become the chief writer of Eisenhower's farewell address, recalled in an oral history that Cousins had done some writing for Eisenhower in the first term, calling him a "more sensitive, but very beautiful writer."[4] But no draft or correspondence over a speech can be found in Cousins's papers or the Eisenhower Library. In 1959, Eisenhower invited Cousins to submit a speech on the subject of getting the world of nations to obey a uniform set of laws; it was drafted but not delivered. Still, Eisenhower sometimes used his correspondence with Cousins in his speechwriting process. In November 1957, in the wake of the Soviet Sputnik launch, Eisenhower's staff was working on an address about science, space exploration, and ballistic missiles. According to his secretary's notes, the president phoned Secretary of State Dulles to say "he was unhappy with the draft of speech [Arthur] Larson sent down. . . . The President referred to a full page article that Norman Cousins and a group are going to publish—and he thinks a little of that idealism ought to go in this speech."[5] When the United States launched its own satellite in early 1958, there was considerable discussion among White House staff about using a draft speech Cousins had submitted on the subject of using outer space exploration only for peaceful purposes.

Eisenhower's consultations with Cousins did not turn him into a nuclear pacifist. The administration continued to build and test nuclear weapons, and Eisenhower continued to believe that many of the issues around nuclear fallout could be solved technologically. Moreover, the relationship sometimes grew contentious, especially when Cousins's opinions highlighted the unwanted consequences of America's continued reliance on a nuclear arsenal. In 1957 there was increasing public concern over the issues of nuclear fallout and a nuclear test ban. Cousins had persuaded Dr. Albert Schweitzer—the Nobel Peace Prize winner who had famously devoted his life to serving the poor—to issue a "Declaration of Conscience," condemning the health dangers of radioactive fallout and encouraging nuclear powers to enact a ban on future tests. In April 1957, the eighty-two-year-old humanitarian issued the declaration over Radio Oslo, stressing the genetic harm caused by fallout and concluding, "We are forced to regard every increase in the existing danger through further creation of radioactive elements by atom bomb explosions as a catastrophe for the human race, a catastrophe that must be prevented under every circumstance."[6] (Coincidentally, a radioactive rain, the result of Soviet nuclear tests, fell over Norway as Schweitzer's statement was being read.)

Although Schweitzer's warning was not broadcast in the United States, it was reported in a front-page *New York Times* article and provoked a response from Willard Libby, the chairman of the Atomic Energy Commission, who argued that nuclear fallout was a small price to pay for American freedom.[7] This became a highly controversial position, but it more or less represented administration policy. Two years earlier, the president's Science Advisory Committee had concluded: "The public will need indoctrination to accustom themselves to the fact that low levels of radiation can and must be lived with. Radiation must be a phenomenon that is universally accepted and understood."[8]

Acceptance was not easily achieved. Fallout became an even greater flash point after estimates from the British Atomic Scientists Association circulated that nuclear tests were creating thousands of leukemia cases a year. An opinion poll in May 1957 found that 63 percent of Americans favored banning nuclear tests. *Newsweek* maintained: "Not since Hiroshima had such a bitter and fateful debate raged over the building, testing and ultimate use of the A-bomb—and its vastly more destructive offspring, the H-bomb. Governments, scientists, military men, just plain citizens—all are caught up in the controversy."[9]

The government became defensive, and a campaign began to criticize those who were pushing the fallout issue. Scientific claims were clouded by counterclaims, the credentials of the critics were called into question, and Libby insisted the bottom line was that continued nuclear tests were required "for the survival of our Nation and that of the free world." This squabble prompted Cousins to write again to Eisenhower, who answered that "while I carry on energetically the program I believe we must pursue at this moment to provide for the security of our country, I am working unceasingly for the time when war itself will be eliminated and the atomic danger will be a thing of the past."[10]

"One Small Ball"

The launch of the Sputnik satellite on October 4, 1957, hit the Eisenhower White House like a targeted missile. Whether it represented a scientific breakthrough for the Soviet Union is a matter that can still be debated. But as a public relations coup, it unsettled the administration more than any other event, including the *Brown vs. Board of Education* decision of 1954. The president set a defiant tone with his insistence that the first Sputnik launch was but "one small ball" thrust into the sky.

All the unresolved debates over military budgets and readiness resurfaced with a nagging urgency. To the knowledgeable, the Sputnik launch implied that the Soviets now had the ability to hitch a nuclear warhead to a missile and launch it thousands of miles from their own soil, thus ushering in an expensive and disruptive new phase of the arms race in which they had the lead. The White House's advisors estimated that by as early as 1959, as a contemporary press account put it, "the U.S.S.R. could deploy enough intercontinental-range ballistic missiles to smash or paralyze the Strategic Air Command's U.S. bases. The attack could occur with a warning of no more than ten or fifteen minutes."[11]

While the public was focused on the two Sputnik launches, Washington's elite was arguably more devastated by the release of an exceptionally well-timed panel study—delivered four days after the second Sputnik orbit—that appeared to show the Soviet military threat was even greater than the administration thought. Entitled "Deterrence & Survival in the Nuclear Age," it was known informally as the Gaither Report, after its panel chairman, H. Rowan Gaither of the RAND Corporation. The report—classified top secret—cited "spectacular progress" in Soviet military development after World War II. The Soviets, the authors claimed, had enough fissionable material for fifteen hundred atomic weapons and had "probably surpassed" the United States in the production of nuclear-tipped intercontinental missiles. They proposed a massive military spending program that would not only match the alleged Soviet offensive capabilities but commit more than $20 billion to a nationwide system of nuclear fallout shelters.

In the panic that ensued after the report's conclusions became known, many public figures—Democratic politicians especially, but also among others the nuclear physicist Edward Teller—compared the Sputnik launch to Pearl Harbor. Lyndon Johnson, the Senate majority leader, declared that "the Russians have beaten us at our own game—daring scientific advances in the nuclear age." Senator John F. Kennedy would make Sputnik a major issue in his 1958 re-election campaign. Demands for an American response—at a minimum, having the president appoint a "missile czar"—were nearly overwhelming. An unnamed presidential advisor was quoted in *Fortune* as saying: "That week after the first Sputnik was one prolonged nightmare. Any number of people—from the Pentagon, from State, and from the Hill—were dashing in and out of the President's office. Each new visitor had a longer face than the one before."[12]

The political fallout was considerable. Democrats on Capitol Hill were keen to find a scapegoat, and the Eisenhower administration's earlier insistence on balancing military expenditures with fiscal restraint could easily, in panicked retrospect, be made to look as if the administration allowed itself to be outflanked by the Soviets. True or not, having to expend energy and political capital to defend against such charges robbed Eisenhower of his greatest political credential: his monopoly on issues of national security. As the White House prepared its responses, Arthur Larson wrote to fellow staffers: "More comments are reaching me on the Sputnick [*sic*] business . . . these from friends. Reaction of bewilderment is shifting to anger . . . DDE's prestige in his special area is slipping . . . I am amazed at the extent and depth of these reactions as I pick up my contacts around the country."[13]

Despite the considerable pressure, neither the president nor his most important advisors were moved to make fundamental policy shifts. Everything that could be done to launch a satellite was put into place, and missile budgets were increased. (But not as much as some within the administration wished; Eisenhower was concerned that bumping up missile-related spending too high in the 1959 budget would "lead people to say that nothing had been done in the last five years.")[14] But in general, the administration did whatever it could, short of releasing confidential data from U-2 spy planes, to convey that it did not share the conclusions of the Gaither Report. Internally, it took the stance that attacks on the Defense Department and calls for more military spending were politically motivated—a White House military aide referred to the "Democratic Agitation Cabal"—and that budgetary restraint remained a vital priority.

"An Unwarranted Part"

The period following the Sputnik-Gaither crisis demon-strates Eisenhower's military-industrial-complex critique in its early stages. Still, who was behind the faulty intel-ligence and calls for military buildup in the Gaither Re-port? The leadership consisted of known and trusted Eisenhower advisors, but there could be no hiding the fact that the billions in increased military spending called for by the panel would benefit many of the very people making the recommendations. Two of the report's princi-pal directors were Robert C. Sprague, who headed his own business of military electronics, and William C. Fos-ter of the Olin-Mathiesen Chemical Company, a pro-ducer of gunpowder and ammunition.

From the studies he had conducted for the Army in the 1930s, Eisenhower was keenly aware of the interdepen-dency between the military and private industry. And while he believed that protecting the American economy and private enterprise was a critical mission for the mili-tary, that goal also involved ensuring that the military and the economy had to be restrained from merging into a behemoth that could threaten both. As early as Decem-ber 1954, according to one account, Eisenhower lectured his defense secretary and the Joint Chiefs of Staff about the dangers of military-industrial largesse. Harold Stassen, who served the Eisenhower administration in a number of capacities, recalls the president saying that

> in view of the joint importance of our economic
> strength and our military strength, our military
> establishment must take on some responsibility for
> our economic strength. We must have a dynamic
> industrial base. But the industrial base must never
> dominate our military establishment, nor should
> it be the other way around. And this is extremely
> important—and I'm not sure anyone can see down
> the road far enough at this stage—if the military and
> our industry leaders ever team up, they can dictate the
> whole country. And they will end up with too much
> power. And that will be bad. . . . The entire military
> establishment must stand firm against greed, against
> corruption, against narrow favoritism, and against
> monopoly. There's a real danger of the military
> ganging up with powerful industrial leaders, and
> parceling out the contracts for weapons and research
> and all kinds of products and services. Bigness means
> lots of money to hand out—and that's dangerous,
> dangerous.[15]

By the time of the Sputnik-Gaither frenzy, it could be argued that just such a situation had come to pass, and Eisenhower glimpsed it in what might seem an unlikely venue—trade journals catering to the aerospace industry. Titles like *Aviation Week* and *Air Force* magazine were scarcely more than a decade old, yet they were helping set the tone of public debate over security policy. Like congressional hearings controlled by Democrats, these publications became a venue for the largely unfiltered views of the military establishment. They were often harshly, even personally critical of Eisenhower and his Defense Department managers.

Shortly after the Sputnik launch, for example, *Aviation Week* editorialized that Americans

> have a right to know the facts about the relative position of the U.S. and the Soviet Union in this technological race which is perhaps the most significant single event of our times. They have the right to find out why a nation with our vastly superior scientific, economic and military potential is being at the very least equaled and perhaps being surpassed by a country that less than two decades ago couldn't even play in the same scientific ball park. They also have a right to make the decisions as to whether they want their government to maintain our current leadership of the free world regardless of the cost in dollars and sweat, or whether they wish to supinely abdicate this position in favor of enjoying a few more years of the hedonistic prosperity that now enfolds our country. These are choices the citizens of this land must make for themselves. They are not decisions to be made arbitrarily by a clique of leaders in an ivory tower or on a golf course.[16]

But perhaps more mesmerizing than the magazines' editorial content was their advertising. To flip through these publications in the late 1950s was to peer into an otherwise hidden America, where prosperity and security seemed to orbit solely around a single vast and growing industry. Aviation in 1957 was approximately an $11 billion business, with giants like Boeing, Douglas Aircraft, and General Dynamics bringing in more than $1 billion each in annual revenue. (IBM that year had revenues of $734 million and General Motors about $10.8 billion.) Nearly all of that revenue came from military contracts, and these magazines were where military contractors hawked their goods. There were also ads for the raw materials needed to make planes and rockets: titanium, graphite, rubber, stainless steel, aluminum. Layered on top of that were dozens of subindustries that had sprung up after the war, many of which straddled the line between public subsidy and private enterprise: makers of helicopters, circuit breakers, aircraft bolts, aircraft engines, roller bearings, navigation and radar systems, aircraft spark plugs, rockets, and much else. A typical full-page ad from January 1957, for example, hawks a product made by the Radio Corporation of America—RCA, at the time, the twenty-fifth-largest company in America, with nearly eighty thousand employees and well over a billion dollars in annual revenue. Most Americans associated it with radios and televisions, but—as this ad made clear— RCA also had a "defense electronic products" division that made guidance systems for Air Force planes. An illustration shows seven white Air Force fighters, each with its system trained on a large, black, unmarked aircraft. The copy promises readers, "Fire control radar tells WHERE TO AIM/WHEN TO FIRE!"

It's not hard to view such an ad as a company using a sense of military insecurity to sell its product. Nor is it hard to imagine the Eisenhower White House—whose attempts to control military spending were constantly under attack—viewing such material with outrage and disbelief. Most advertising, after all, seeks to sell a product or service to multiple customers. For leading-edge military products with national security implications, there was only one customer—the Pentagon.

These journals were viewed with irritated fascination by the Eisenhower White House, and particularly by Malcolm Moos. In an interview, Moos recalled the trade publications specifically in the context of the farewell speech, noting that Peter Aurand, a naval attaché whose father had been a classmate of Eisenhower's at West Point, would "bring in these aerospace journals, talk about them, leave them on my desk. And it's astounding to go through them and see some 25,000 different kinds of related companies in this thing."[17] Eisenhower's scientific advisor James Killian said that the president could not stomach the journals and their ads: "Repeatedly, I saw Ike angered by the excesses, both in text and advertising, of the aerospace-electronics press, which advocated ever bigger and better weapons to meet an ever bigger and better Soviet threat they had conjured up."[18]

Eisenhower raised the issue himself in a press conference the day after his farewell speech: "I did point out last evening that some of this misuse of influence and power could come about unwittingly but just by the very nature of the thing, when you see almost every one of your magazines, no matter what they are advertising, has a picture of the Titan missile or the Atlas or solid fuel or other things, there is becoming a great influence, almost an insidious penetration of our own minds that the only thing this country is engaged in is weaponry and missiles. And, I'll tell you we just can't afford to do that. The reason we have them is to protect the great values in which we believe, and they are far deeper even than our own lives and our own property, as I see it."[19]

By 1959 Eisenhower had begun to see private military contractors as self-interested, malign actors in the budget process. In a June meeting with legislative leaders about defense appropriations, he questioned an additional $85 million that had been put into the ATLAS program, an early intercontinental ballistic missile. Congressman Gerald Ford tried to reassure him with a variety of explanations: the Air Force had recently revised its cost estimates; the increase was much less than what many in Congress were proposing; other parts of the missiles appropriation had been reduced. But Eisenhower was not persuaded. According to the meeting notes, "The President protested the political pressures that the munitions industry brings to bear on the Congress, and especially the resort to full-page advertisements such as that by Boeing in regard to the BOMARC. He thought it was clear that other elements than the basic defense of the country were entered into the handling of these problems."[20]

This outburst was sufficiently unusual that it was almost immediately leaked to the press; the *New York Times* compared Eisenhower's position to that of the Nye "munitions inquiry" of the 1930s. A *Times* reporter wrote that Eisenhower had let it be known that he "believed political and financial influences rather than military considerations alone were playing an unwarranted part in the defense debate." It was evidently a presidential theme in 1959. Killian's memoir notes that later that month, while discussing an upcoming Space Council meeting and the need for better coordination and single management of national missile ranges, Eisenhower insisted: "We must avoid letting the munitions companies dictate the pattern of our organization."[21]

It was not only military contractors who were challenging Eisenhower's conduct of military policy. Increasingly in 1958 and 1959, he became frustrated and annoyed at the incompetence, disloyalty, and outright insubordination he perceived among military officials ostensibly under his command. This frustration could take many forms. In June 1959, the administration faced a proliferating and often overlapping system of missile and aircraft defenses: different agencies developed pet programs, with little centralized planning around overall strategic needs. A choice needed to be made between the Nike-Hercules missile and the Bomarc B missile, each with different strengths and weaknesses, and different requirements for use in conjunction with bombers. In a meeting with his technical advisors, the president "said it is to him an indication of weakness in the top leadership of the Defense Department when a choice between two weapon systems comes to the President for resolution. He felt that this type of problem should be settled in the Defense Department."[22] In a related discussion about interagency coordination of strategic policy a month later, the president said "he cannot figure out what is causing the trouble in the Joint Chiefs of Staff. The organization seems to be failing to do its job."[23]

These concerns were expressed with other people in the room. In the summer of 1958, the administration was badly outmaneuvered by Congress over the issue of spending on atomic energy. The Senate passed a bill in mid-July authorizing nearly $387 million in spending on a variety of atomic reactor design and construction projects, nearly twice what the administration wanted. Congressional Democrats had been pushing hard to increase the nation's plutonium production, exposing a turf war between the Defense Department and the Atomic Energy Commission over who would control the production facilities. The Joint Chiefs of Staff had repeatedly requested more plutonium, but the AEC had balked. When Eisenhower realized the bind this put him in, he phoned a Defense Department official and, as his secretary recorded the conversation, "complained in salty language about the laxity in the Defense forces—he said he would have, if he had done some of the things that [they] have done in the last few days, shot himself. The Plutonium incident (the AEC has said they do not need more plutonium, the Chiefs say they do), he either embarrasses one group or the other, or he signs the bill. The President suggested firing a few people—and said that people in the service either ought to obey orders or get the hell out of the service."[24]

In late 1959, the administration had decided to stop developing the B-70 bomber as a replacement for the B-52, feeling that by the time the plane actually became available in the mid-to-late 1960s, advances in Soviet anti-aircraft weapons would eliminate its high-altitude advantage. This reversal was denounced by Senator Clair Engle, a Democrat from California (where some of the bomber's design and manufacturing facilities were located), and in January 1960, Air Force Chief of Staff Thomas White announced that he would testify before a congressional committee in favor of restoring the bomber program.[25]

Eisenhower, who believed his role as commander-in-chief required that military officials support his position in public, was incensed. He telephoned Defense Secretary Thomas S. Gates, clearly trying to figure out whether White should or could be dismissed. Eisenhower "said that ever since the days of the Fair Deal and the New Deal, discipline had been lost in the high ranking officers of the services. Nothing does he deplore more. Everyone seems to think he has a compulsion to tell in public his personal views. The President went on to say that there used to be an item in efficiency reports that asked whether, once a decision had been [made], the officer in question carried it out without question. That question was deleted by the 'psychologists.' The President would like to see it put back."[26] Tellingly, both John F. Kennedy and Richard Nixon would support the B-70 bomber in that year's presidential campaign.

"Apathetic Complacency"

Given his frustration with his military subordinates—to say nothing of congressional Democrats and the ever-uncooperative Soviets—it is not surprising that Eisenhower began to indulge his more idealistic side in searching for solutions. Some were halfhearted notions that served as little more than propaganda. In July 1960, for example, he proposed a worldwide plebiscite in which citizens of all countries would vote on whether they would prefer to live in a Communist or non-Communist society.[27]

Other ideas received deeper consideration. In his last years in the White House he began to entertain nonmilitary approaches to security more seriously and consistently than any time since his 1953 "Chance for Peace" address. At the beginning of 1958, he and his staff embarked on a plan to mark the fifth anniversary of that speech with another address before the same group, the American Society of Newspaper Editors. Eisenhower wanted to accomplish a few major goals: to point out that the United States had been involved in no protracted wars since 1953; to remind Americans how much they lose through massive military expenditures; and to seek new proposals for how peace might be achieved by nonmilitary means.

Informing the last category was the notion that the United States would have to accept that the Soviet Union would have a Communist government for the foreseeable future and, instead of seeking to change that, find new ways of coexisting with it. Eisenhower latched onto the idea of a large-scale student exchange program, whereby ten thousand Russian students would spend a year in American universities. (A much smaller exchange program had begun a few years earlier.)[28] The reasoning, Eisenhower explained to his brother, was that he was "tired of working with mature men already set in their prejudices" and thought that allowing younger, more flexible Russian minds to experience America might convince some that the American way was superior.[29]

Not everyone in government favored this proposal (although FBI chief J. Edgar Hoover—who might reasonably have been alarmed at the security implications of importing thousands of Communist-affiliated students— apparently endorsed the idea in a conversation with the president). In a two-page shootdown that is a classic expression of bureaucratic inertia, a State Department memorandum listed all the problems with publicly proposing the idea: the Soviets might not accept it; neither universities nor the attorney general seemed likely to accept responsibility for the Russian students; many American universities were located in places where Soviet nationals were not allowed to travel; American universities were already crowded and turning away qualified American students; other nations, particularly Soviet satellite nations like Poland and Yugoslavia, would feel slighted if Soviet students were accepted in larger numbers than theirs; and so on.

Even so, Eisenhower seemed for a time to think he was on to a big idea, and he planned to make it the centerpiece of the ASNE speech. The drafts that went back and forth between Larson and Eisenhower spoke of a "new and great experiment" in which "all mankind should profit if the young men and women of the Soviet Union and the United States can learn in sympathetic association the problems, the possibilities, the resources and the rewards of a common destiny in a world where time and space no longer isolate the nations."[30] While the draft did not say how many students would be involved, it did express the "hope that several thousand could accept." In a deft diplomatic gesture, the speech did not require anything from the Soviets other than their selection of qualified students to participate; if the Soviets wished to reciprocate with a similar program, it would be welcome but voluntary.

That portion of the speech was never delivered, perhaps because of the State Department's objections, perhaps because—as he indicated to his staff—Eisenhower was not confident that the speech had enough new ideas. Instead, he spoke to the ASNE group about the need to reorganize the military. Still, the draft speech reflects Eisenhower's careful personal consideration; he wrote to Dulles three times about it, and at one point he instructed his assistant that he should not be disturbed while working on it. The proposed speech's return to the themes and idealism of "Chance for Peace" makes parts of it read like notes for the farewell address. Eisenhower referred to the "appalling costs" of security obtained through armaments and said that since his 1953 speech, the country had spent more than $200 billion on its military—not including foreign aid—with "scarcely any contribution to the constructive purpose of mankind." In a peaceful world, that money could have "financed our entire highway program, built all the hospitals needed in the next decade, provided money for every worthwhile hydro-electric project programmed by our experts, allocated some 10 billions a year for security forces," and still allowed the country to reduce the national debt.

The draft speech would have gone on to discuss the student exchange and other ways in which the need for military spending might be reduced. But before that, Eisenhower was prepared to introduce a new factor behind wasteful military spending: the "lack of stability in defensive strength." The idea was that military spending was unreliable because it was tied to urgent-seeming fads. "Too often the security of our country has thoughtlessly been made the victim of political trends, currently popular. A wave of fear sweeping over the country can cause us to spend far more than needed at the moment." Equally damaging were periods of "apathetic complacency" when the military was starved, encouraging attack and requiring hasty buildups later. It was clear which period Eisenhower thought he was living through: "The expense of any useless duplication in procedure, any needless unit of strength or obsolescence in quality is an additional cost not merely during the particular year, but during all these years stretching out ahead of us until correction is made. . . . If we are wasteful, blindly foolish or negligent, our security will be jeopardized and the costs may be such as to compel governmental controls incompatible with the freedoms we cherish." Even though it was not delivered, the speech sounded a theme that neither Eisenhower nor his staff would forget.

FIVE

The Speech

There are conflicting accounts of how Eisenhower came
to utter the phrase "military-industrial complex." Most of
his biographers spend only a page or two discussing the
genesis of his farewell address, even while acknowledging
that it is, as Blanche Wiesen Cook put it, "the most important statement of his career."[1]

One biographer, Stephen Ambrose, suggested that the
very idea for the speech came not from someone within
the White House or Eisenhower's circle of advisors but
from Norman Cousins. Ambrose wrote that on December
14, 1960, Eisenhower's personal secretary, Ann Whitman,
"typed up a note and sent it into the Oval Office. 'Norman Cousins called,' she told the President. 'His sugges-

tion: that you give a "farewell" address to the country . . . reviewing your Administration, telling of your hopes for the future. A great, sweeping document.'"[2] Eisenhower then, wrote Ambrose, put speechwriter Malcolm Moos onto the task over the next month. But while Cousins certainly affected Eisenhower's views about war, peace, and nuclear weapons, other evidence shows that he had little if any influence on Eisenhower's decision to give a farewell speech, or on its content.

Other biographers offer tidbits of how the phrase was developed. Geoffrey Perret writes that Eisenhower "originally intended to include Congress in this indictment and deliver a blast at the 'military-industrial-congressional complex.' At the last minute, he struck out 'congressional.' It wasn't for a President to berate Congress any more than it was his business to berate the Supreme Court."[3] Douglas Brinkley, on the other hand, tells us that Moos's original draft of the speech, completed "shortly before Christmas" in 1960, "cautioned against a 'military-industrial-scientific complex,' but at the urging of Eisenhower's science advisor, James Killian, it was shortened to the now-famous phrase."[4] This too is undocumented: the seven extant drafts do not have anything else (such as "scientific" or "congressional") attached to the phrase "military-industrial complex." At a minimum, if such phrases existed in any drafts, they were not changed "at the last minute."

These errors are understandable, given that the written record of the speech's evolution is frustratingly incomplete. It is almost certain that Eisenhower and his advisors hashed over its major themes in conversations that left no documentary trace. Their deliberations have sometimes been reconstructed by participants well after the events. Even in the best of circumstances, these participants may not have been fully aware that they were touching only one part of the elephant. Thus it is worth reviewing what the historical record does reveal.[5]

"I Want To Have a Message"

Few historians have remarked that Eisenhower embraced the idea of giving a sweeping farewell speech years before he chose its theme. Why this notion appealed to him is not hard to fathom: it allowed him to put a closing parenthesis on eight difficult years in office by speaking directly to the American people without the filter of Congress or the press. Unlike unscripted press conferences, in which Eisenhower's uneven syntax often made him appear rambling, a farewell address would give him a chance to influence the nation's future agenda clearly and effectively.

Malcolm Moos, who joined the White House speechwriting staff in 1958, recalled in an oral history that "some two years before he left office," the president "was in a philosophical mood one day, and turned to me and said, 'By the way, Malcolm, I want to have something to say when I leave here, and I want you to be thinking about it.' He said, 'I'm not interested in capturing headlines, but I want to have a message and I want you to be thinking about it well in advance.'"[6] The occasion for this comment, Moos said, was that he had shown the president a book of presidential addresses, which noted that Alexander Hamilton had drafted Washington's farewell address.

By May of 1959 there is evidence of preliminary planning for an Eisenhower valedictory speech. In that month, an unofficial group of advisors (including Moos) met at the home of Milton Eisenhower, the president's brother. There they laid out an agenda for thirteen speeches that the president should make before his departure from office. Discussing this plan in a letter to his brother, Eisenhower wrote: "I have, as yet, no fixed idea that I should deliver a so-called 'farewell' talk to the Congress, even if that body should invite me to do so. The reason I have been toying with this idea is because of my experience— which by that time will have extended to a full six years— in working with a Congress controlled by the opposite political party. Needless to say, there would be no profit in expressing, in such a setting, anything that was partisan in character. Rather I think the purpose would be to emphasize a few homely truths that apply to the responsibilities and duties of a government that must be responsive to the will of majorities, even when the decisions of those majorities create apparent paradoxes."[7]

The speech he ultimately delivered bore little relation to that theme. The earliest indication of the actual subject of the farewell address is in a "memorandum for file," dated October 31, 1960, and prepared by Ralph E. Williams, a Navy captain who worked with Eisenhower's speechwriting staff. On that morning, says the memo, Williams and Moos discussed two themes for the president's 1961 State of the Union address. The second theme, later discarded, was the "world wide tendency for orderly societies to break down into mob ridden anarchies." But the first remained remarkably intact: "The problem of militarism—for the first time in its history, the United States has a permanent war-based industry—aircraft, 90%—missiles, 100%, etc. Not only that but flag and general officers retiring at an early age take positions in war based industrial complex shaping its decisions and guiding the direction of its tremendous thrust. This creates a danger that what the Communists have always said about us may become true. We must be very careful to insure that the 'merchants of death do not come to dictate national policy.'"[8]

Frustratingly, the memorandum does not say who came up with the phrase "war based industrial complex." There is no suggestion that it originated with Eisenhower—although as recounted in the previous chapter, this theme was close to his heart—and neither Moos nor Williams would claim it consistently. In a 1988 oral history, Williams referred to it as "my original thought off the top of my head," and directly took credit for changing "war based" to "military." But in a 1985 letter to the Eisenhower Library, he said that the October 31 memo was written *after* ideas had been hashed out with Moos and aide Stephen Hess—so the original phrase could have been someone else's. Moos, for his part, seemed content to let people believe he had coined it. He proudly told at least two interviewers that the Library of Congress had told him that its researchers spent two years searching unsuccessfully for a precedent for the phrase.[9] But he never, to my knowledge, explicitly said it was his.

Williams uses the 1930s catchphrase "merchants of death" in his memorandum and puts it in quotation marks. There are different ways to interpret this. Perhaps Williams wished to distance himself from an inflammatory phrase, or perhaps he was directly quoting Moos, a political scientist and former journalist who once described his politics as "left-wing Republicanism." Moos had written about the disarmament movement of the 1920s and 1930s in a 1954 book called *Power Through Purpose: The Realism of Idealism as a Basis for Foreign Policy*. That book, cowritten with Thomas I. Cook, contains at least one passage that strongly foreshadows Eisenhower's farewell address: "We have to decide on the proper balance between peacetime industry, normal consumption, desirable investment, and enjoyment of leisure, on the one hand, and the urgencies of immediate defense and lasting preparedness, on the other. . . . We quite properly insist that it would grievously harm us without helping others if we were to ruin our economy, destroy our material welfare, and sacrifice our future development in an attempt to meet fully all the economic and military needs of all present or future allies, whether those needs are measured by their present distance from our own standards and accomplishments or by some lesser criterion of adequacy based on the achievements of Western industrial society."[10] It appears that Moos had ready at hand the arguments, and some of the rhetoric, for a speech about excessive military influence.

Williams's mention of early military retirees working for military contractors is also an intriguing ripple. Eisenhower's actual speech does not mention this, nor do any extant drafts. But it was clearly a concern, at least to Moos. Discussing the origins of the speech, he told an oral historian: "I had a student who was working on a study that I'd suggested on the number of people that were retiring from the armed forces at relatively young ages, in their forties and things, and becoming directors of industries, aerospace industries particularly, from the Air Force, the Navy, the Army."[11]

If any copy of this study was used in preparing the speech, it does not exist in the archives. Still, the notion of a revolving door between the military and its contractors was part of the merchants of death thesis back in the 1930s; by the late 1950s it operated on a much larger scale and in peacetime. It's curious that Moos felt the need to cite a student's work on this topic, since it had been the subject of formal congressional inquiry at least twice in the 1950s. In 1956, a subcommittee of the House Armed Services Committee looked into how the Air Force awarded contracts and found that the vast majority were negotiated rather than subjected to competitive bids. The investigation mushroomed into an attack on the high salaries and profits earned by aircraft companies that did business with the Air Force, including such prominent firms as Fairchild Engine and Airplane Corporation and McDonnell Aircraft Corporation. Members of Congress alleged that since the overwhelming majority of business done by large aircraft companies was by government contract, these firms were effectively "subsidiaries" of the federal government. One figure singled out for criticism was General Joseph T. McNarney, who in 1952 took a $75,000-a-year job as president of the company that made the B-36 bomber, which he had controversially supported in 1949. Curiously, McNarney told a congressional committee that he was hired after Senator Stuart Symington (a former head of the Air Force) gave him an unidentified phone number and told him to call it and inquire about a job. Another firm was attacked for charging the government a million dollars to produce advertising.

The second inquiry took place in the summer of 1959, the same time that Eisenhower was complaining in meetings about the influence of the munitions industry. It was not always fruitful; Vice Admiral Hyman Rickover reluctantly gave a House subcommittee a confidential list of former officers who supposedly tried to influence him from new posts at defense contracting firms, but this led to no major revelations. An executive from Martin Aircraft Company admitted that his firm had flown high-ranking military officials—including the chairman of the Joint Chiefs of Staff and the secretaries of the Air Force and Navy—to the Bahamas for weekend parties. By January 1960, a House investigating committee had revealed that the nation's hundred largest military contractors— which received 80 percent of new weapons contracts— employed 762 former military officers with rank of colonel (or captain in the Navy) or above. The committee recommended a two-year ban on any form of selling by all officers or civilians leaving the Department of Defense.[12]

Eisenhower and his speechwriters thus came late to the game in identifying the corrupting potential of military contracting and lobbying practices. The most plausible explanation for why they did not take up this issue earlier is political. The congressional inquiries were all conducted by Democrats (mostly southern conservative Democrats), in the context of bitter budgetary battles with the administration. Their goal was not solely to reform procurement and contracting but also to paint the administration and top military brass as incompetent stewards of the nation's defense. Going at least as far back as the 1956 Senate hearings over air power—which promulgated the idea of a "bomber gap" and a "missile gap" a year before Sputnik—the Democratic position was consistently that Eisenhower and his appointees were not spending enough money on the military, and not spending it wisely.

In early November, as Richard Nixon and John F. Kennedy campaigned for the presidency, Moos and Williams continued to work on the farewell speech. "Around the first week of November," Moos recalled, he gave Eisenhower a draft, and after a few days the president said to him, "I think you've got something here." Moos said that Milton Eisenhower also had a hand in the speech, as he did with most major speeches.

The next few weeks in the White House were somewhat chaotic, as Army trucks loaded up Eisenhower's personal possessions to be hauled off to the presidential library in Abilene. At this stage, Moos and Williams had little role in shaping the speech, but it does not appear from the record that either of the Eisenhowers made major changes to the original text, and certainly the president had his hands full with the transition to the next administration. The extant drafts of the speech are dated between January 6 and 16, and they show only minor textual changes. Those drafts represent an incomplete record of any back and forth that might have existed between the Eisenhower brothers, or anyone else they may have consulted privately. Yet according to the speechwriters, they do not deviate significantly from what Moos and Williams originally drafted. Commenting on how well the speech captured Eisenhower's own views, Williams said: "Apparently it was what he wanted to say because he made so few changes to it."[13]

There was some internal debate about whether the speech should be delivered before Congress but, according to Moos, the president rejected this idea, arguing that it was the content of the speech that mattered. In Moos's words, Eisenhower "was striving to reach tomorrow's conscience, not today's headlines."[14]

Eisenhower was never entirely comfortable with the medium of television, and after his stroke he was apt to garble the pronunciation of words or forget them altogether. Television cameras were brought into the Oval Office, with their thicket of massive electric cables strewn across the carpet. Maroon felt was taped to the president's desk to reduce the glare from the lights aimed at his head.

The military-industrial complex was of course only a small part of a broader speech. Eisenhower also warned against other undesirable aspects of a federal government growing in scale and influence. In particular, he identified technology and research as areas where dependence on government funds could be a pernicious force. The expensive technology needed for cutting-edge research had made government funding almost a necessity. "In holding scientific research and discovery in respect, as we should, we must also be alert to the equal and opposite danger that public policy could itself become the captive of a scientific-technological elite." More typically, he warned against excessive government spending and debt: "As we peer into society's future, we—you and I, and our government—must avoid the impulse to live only for today, plundering for our own ease and convenience the precious resources of tomorrow. We cannot mortgage the material assets of our grandchildren without risking the loss also of their political and spiritual heritage." And he echoed some of the idealistic rhetoric of the "Chance for Peace" speech: "Disarmament, with mutual honor and confidence, is a continuing imperative. Together we must learn how to compose differences, not with arms, but with intellect and decent purpose." Eisenhower gave himself credit for not creating any new wars but registered his disappointment at not creating a genuine peace.

What Did He Mean?

What Eisenhower *didn't* say also deserves mention. Though consistent in many ways with the merchants of death idea, the farewell speech stopped well short of saying that arms and other military contractors start, encourage, or prolong wars so as to increase profits. Rather, the risks Eisenhower saw are more in the area of debt created through massive military spending, and in the curtailment of individual and economic liberty. Both of those ideas, long-standing concerns of his, would take on great significance after Eisenhower left office. While many would come to adopt the stance that military spending both stimulated the American economy and forced the Soviets to drain their resources in order to compete, Eisenhower's warning focused on the negative side of the war economy thesis: left to its own devices, the MIC would bankrupt America.

As soon as he had finished the speech, historians and rhetoricians began asking what he really meant. Determining the meaning of spoken words is an endless, elusive task, complicated even further in this case by the involvement of speechwriters.

It is an essential part of crafting a political speech that speechwriters attempt to capture the thinking and expressive style of the person for whom they are writing. Part of that process means poring over past speeches, articles, testimony, and other public statements. Ralph Williams's memorandum of October 31 included a self-reminder to "analyze previous major addresses of DDE." Of course Eisenhower, like other presidents, had considerable say over the words he would ultimately deliver. The Eisenhower archives are filled with multiple drafts of earlier speeches containing the president's scrawled amendments, as well as memoranda indicating a need to beef up particular portions of planned addresses. When a draft was delivered to the president, he would often send it by messenger to his brother Milton, who would rewrite it overnight, though with an eye more toward structure than theme. "Seldom did I add new material, for I did not possess it at my residence," Milton wrote in a memoir. "I nearly always rewrote the speech completely, giving it a normal progression in fact and thought and easily using the President's own phrases which were not different from my own." Only then, Milton asserted, would the president begin making his own revisions—on a freshly typed, triple-spaced draft—"and when he had finished one would have thought that a dozen chickens with dirty feet had found delight in scratching on every page."[15]

The chicken-scratching that survives on the farewell address is relatively minimal, but nonetheless it is clear that Eisenhower had taken ownership of the concept of a military-industrial complex by the time he delivered the speech. By that point he had had nearly two months to consider it. As Williams put it: "I'm sure the President never thought about either the phrase or the concept itself until Mac Moos put the first draft under his nose. I am equally sure . . . that it struck a responsive chord in his breast. Ike may not have always said the right things, but he never put anything into a formal speech that he didn't believe and fully intend to say."[16]

As for exactly why this concept appealed to Eisenhower, Williams offers this explanation: "My own belief was that he had been stung by the Democratic candidates' criticism of the 'missile gap' during the 1960 campaign, and the 'bomber gap' in 1956, neither of which had the slightest basis in fact, and outraged at the antics of the cabal consisting of Air Force officers, aviation industry lobbyists and trade associations, and Congressmen promoting arms programs beneficial to their districts who regularly fed ammunition to his critics."[17]

Yet even if Eisenhower's meaning and motivation can be roughly ascertained, they do not sufficiently answer the questions raised by his presentation. He depicted a standing American army and a massive arsenal as necessary— so how is an MIC to be avoided or contained? If the threat was as profound as he laid it out—"economic, political, even spiritual"—why did he wait until he was leaving office to warn the country? If the implication is that even the president of the United States cannot resolve the problem, does that not mean that the MIC already has "unwarranted influence"?

Attempts to answer such questions have contributed to

the durability of the speech and the concept of the MIC. One school of thought that says that when Eisenhower spoke of "peace," he did not mean the cessation of all military activity and planning, and when he spoke of "disarmament," he had no intention of subtracting from America's arsenal or even stopping its growth. While this argument may appear to be mere semantic whittling, it should not be dismissed. Of course the war-scarred general preferred a civilization at peace to one at war, but the Cold War presented a more complex dynamic. There is a plain contradiction between Eisenhower's desire—stated both publicly and privately—for a world at peace, and the fact that the military-industrial complex grew up largely on his watch (although his failure to corral it hardly makes him unique among modern presidents).

Hence, one answer is simple hypocrisy: that Eisenhower said what the country and much of the world wanted to hear, but that as president he had been willing to do whatever was necessary to preserve American military dominance, including using atomic weapons. In a book devoted to the "Atoms for Peace" speech, delivered at the United Nations in December 1953, Ira Chernus has argued that Eisenhower's dovish rhetoric was a deliberate attempt to placate particular audiences and manage the insecurity that arose from his administration's strategic reliance on nuclear weapons. Chernus describes Eisenhower as "haunted" by a nuclear dilemma: in order to preserve peace and security, he had unleashed and enhanced perhaps the most destabilizing military force of all time. A kind of vicious cycle took over in which Eisenhower "would constantly have to demonstrate his commitment to peace in order to enhance the Western alliance's ability and will to fight the cold war."[18] Chernus portrays Eisenhower's mind as an Orwellian arena in which peace could be imagined only in the context of permanent war with an undefeatable enemy.

That dark lens has its uses in analyzing Eisenhower's earlier speeches, but the farewell address, at least on the surface, implies something else, almost an admission that this Orwellian condition exists but that the military-industrial complex is to blame. Eisenhower's lifelong belief in balance had spilled over into critique, because the MIC's resistance to rational management was so great. The speech has a confessional, apologetic aspect: "Disarmament, with mutual honor and confidence, is a continuing imperative. Together we must learn how to compose differences, not with arms, but with intellect and decent purpose. Because this need is so sharp and apparent, I confess that I lay down my official responsibilities in this field with a definite sense of disappointment."

Perhaps a more charitable explanation for the speech's contradictions is that Eisenhower's commitment to peace was lifelong and genuine, but that as president he was hemmed in by advisors and thwarted by Soviet intransigence. There is some evidence for this. The landmark "Chance for Peace" speech of April 1953 went through many drafts, and the more times John Foster Dulles got his hands on it, the more critical of the Soviet Union it became. There are other examples of tonal differences between Dulles and Eisenhower on documents that touched on Soviet relations, with Dulles emphasizing Soviet faults and Eisenhower seeking a more diplomatic common ground. While drafting a document in early 1958, for example, Eisenhower dictated an insert, and then dictated: "I sense a difference with Foster Dulles (in the approach to the Soviets). His is a lawyer's mind. He consistently adheres to a very logical explanation of these difficulties in which we find ourselves with the Soviets and in doing so—with his lawyer's mind—he shows the steps and actions that are bad on their part; and we seek to show that we are doing the decent and just thing. Of course we have got to have a concern and respect for fact and reiteration of official position, but we are likewise trying to 'seek friends and influence people.'"[19] After Dulles's death, in 1959, it was easier for White House speechwriters to "let

Eisenhower be Eisenhower," at least at the level of political rhetoric.

Then again, Eisenhower may simply have changed his mind over time on the crucial question of whether a nuclear arsenal tipped the balance between a military establishment that protected democracy and one that threatened liberty. This is the thinking offered by Geoffrey Perret: "During his eight years in the White House, Eisenhower's views on nuclear weapons changed radically. In 1953, he considered them usable in a wide variety of conflicts. By 1961 he considered them practical in almost none. Their main role was that of a deterrent to Soviet nuclear weapons. Eisenhower had meanwhile become a strong believer in arms control and a nuclear test ban treaty."[20] If nuclear weapons had become useless from a combat point of view, then the bureaucracy and expense necessary to continue producing them were a potential domestic threat.

Taking that reasoning a step further, another explanation is that Eisenhower was contradictory because human beings are often contradictory. Few authors have leaned as heavily on this interpretation as Piers Brendon, who maintains that his own conflicting views of Eisenhower over time "mirror the real paradoxes of the president, the ambiguities of his career, and the countless barely reconcilable facets of his personality, all twinkling like the light from a cut-glass chandelier." Brendon goes so far as to assert that "there is scarcely a single aspect of Ike's life or character about which the evidence is not conflicting or contradictory."[21]

Arguably the most renegade interpretation of the speech is that it is not a warning against the MIC at all. Martin Medhurst has almost certainly written and edited more material on Eisenhower's rhetoric than anyone else, and in an iconoclastic 1994 article he argued that, despite the way that almost everyone has interpreted it, the farewell speech was not a piece of prophecy and that Eisenhower in fact always believed in cooperation between the military and industry. Relying largely on an interview he conducted with Eisenhower's close aide and speechwriter Bryce Harlow, Medhurst portrays the farewell speech as a highly calculated attack on the incoming Kennedy administration—which, he argues, the Eisenhower White House regarded as dangerously naïve on military and economic affairs. The relevant section of the speech is not, in Medhurst's view, "about the military-industrial complex *per se*, but about the ability of future decision makers to utilize that complex in a balanced way, both to protect individual liberties and to prevent the nation as a whole from becoming a garrison state."[22]

Medhurst's argument is provocative but perhaps too narrow in its focus on Kennedy. As Williams's 1985 letter to the Eisenhower Library indicates, Eisenhower felt that congressional Democrats, military contractors, and Air Force officials were just as much at fault in the mismanagement of military spending. Indeed, by the time of the speech Eisenhower had already lost the battle over the arms budget within his own party. Richard Nixon's 1960 campaign did not feel Eisenhower's policy of trying to balance military needs against fiscal restraint could stand up politically against Democratic attacks on the so-called missile gap. Instead, at the urging of Nelson Rockefeller, the 1960 Republican platform offered the military a blank check: "The U.S. can afford and must provide the increased expenditures to implement fully this necessary program for strengthening our defense posture. There must be no price ceiling on America's security."[23]

But the meaning of the speech cannot be located solely in what was intended. Words take on different weight according to how, and by whom, they are received, and those differences can become more pronounced over time. In a letter to a researcher in 1985, Williams acknowledged such shifts, if only to disapprove: "I have always been astonished at the attention that has been given to the 'military-industrial complex' portion of President

Eisenhower's last speech, and agree . . . that its true significance has been distorted beyond recognition. I am sure that had it been uttered by anyone except a President who had been the Army's five-star Chief of Staff it would long since have been forgotten. But as things were, it became red meat for the media, who have gleefully gnawed on it for twenty-five years."[24]

First Reactions

The meaning many Americans would take from Eisenhower's speech depended to a healthy degree on how it was presented in the press. Medhurst has made much of the fact that various media outlets approached it very differently, and that the MIC concept was but one of four ways reporters led off discussing the speech (the others being Eisenhower's warnings about the continued dangers of the Cold War and fight against Communism; his disappointment in failing to achieve an agreement for disarmament; and the need for balance).[25] This is true as far as it goes, but within days the warning about the MIC eclipsed all other interpretations. (Malcolm Moos would refer in a 1964 article simply to "Eisenhower's Farewell Address on the military-industrial complex"—the terms were synonymous.)

For example, Walter Lippmann, whose column "Today

and Tomorrow" was widely syndicated, began his piece on January 18, 1961, by writing: "President Eisenhower's farewell address will be remembered and quoted in the days to come. Rising above the issues which divide the parties and were the material of the election campaign, he dwelt on a question, never before discussed publicly by any responsible official, which is of profound importance to the Nation's future"—which was, of course, the influence of the MIC.[26]

In a press conference the day after the speech, Eisenhower was asked twenty questions, of which two referred to themes from the night before. One, from the *Chicago Daily News*, contrasted his warning about "the dangers to our democratic processes implicit in unparalleled peacetime military establishment" with unspecified criticisms that Eisenhower's own administration had tolerated abuse of executive privilege in the Defense Department. The president dismissed it with a single sentence. The second, from the nonprofit news organization Science Service, concerned what could be done to prevent public policy from being dominated by a scientific-technological elite. After a quick nod to the role of an informed citizenry, Eisenhower made a longer, worried remark about the prevalence of advertising for missiles and weaponry in American magazines. If reporters at the press conference believed that the need for balance or the fight against Communism was the major theme of Eisenhower's address, they apparently saw no need to ask him about it.

By the next Sunday, January 22, *New York Times* reporter Jack Raymond had pulled together a full-page overview of the MIC—replete with bar graphs and pie charts—headlined "The Military-Industrial Complex: An Analysis." Raymond identified several components of the MIC that, while not specifically mentioned by Eisenhower, would later come to be identified with the idea. These included the employment of former military officers by major defense contractors; the size of the defense lobby and its coziness with military leaders; the large portion of scientific research being funded by the Pentagon; the dramatic rise in the military portion of the federal budget, even with the country ostensibly at peace; and Congress's tendency to accede to military requests for more defense spending. Raymond even tipped his hat to the president's concern over the ubiquity of military advertising, noting: "This week, the same issue of The New York Times that carried the report and text of the Eisenhower Budget Message also had a full page advertisement of the merits of an airplane for which no new appropriations were being sought."[27]

What Eisenhower and his speechwriters almost certainly could not have predicted is that his parting words would be most enthusiastically received on the political left, which years before had dismissed him as out-of-touch and a captive of his golf cronies. "It can be said, quite without irony, that nothing became Mr. Eisenhower's career in office like the leaving of it," said an editorial in *The Nation*, which was preparing a series of articles about the influence of the military industry. "For eight years, Mr. Eisenhower has depressed his fellow Americans by a seeming inability to grasp the major problems of his era; but now in the closing days of his Administration he spoke like the statesman and democratic leader we had so long hungered for him to become."[28] Others with a dedicated interest in reducing military spending, including labor leaders and peace activists, would take up the phrase "military-industrial complex" with increasing fervor in coming years, steering the meaning toward their own interpretations.

Interpretations and Embellishments

Many commentators on Eisenhower's speech have concluded that the phrase "military-industrial complex" was
largely ignored until America became deeply entangled
in the Vietnam War. Martin Medhurst argues that it was
rightfully ignored. In his view, to frame the speech as a
warning against the military-industrial complex is a mis-
interpretation, and that for years few did frame it that
way. "Neither in January 1961," he writes, "nor in 1962,
1963, or 1964, indeed at no point prior to the introduction of American ground forces into Vietnam, was Ike's
Farewell understood by most people to be about the dangers of a military-industrial complex. . . . If one examines
the *Reader's Guide to Periodical Literature* from 1961 to

1969, what one finds is that there is no listing at all for the 'military-industrial complex' until 1969. Even individual references to the MIC are rare before the end of the decade."[1]

Alex Roland, another scholar of the MIC, has written less tendentiously: "A survey of *The New York Times* and *The Nation* for the years 1961 to 1990 reveals that the term [military-industrial complex] was little used in the early 1960s. In 1963, the year of Kennedy's assassination, the term did not appear at all in *The New York Times*."[2]

These observations have some validity. The escalation of America's involvement in Vietnam did lead to an increased use of the phrase (and, to give Medhurst his due, no doubt colored the way that history interpreted Eisenhower's speech). Yet this generalization is misleading—and in important instances, factually wrong—because it ignores the robust conversation about the military-industrial complex that preceded the full-scale American involvement in Vietnam. The idea of an overextended military establishment that could threaten, rather than protect, the American way of life was highly significant to many in the early 1960s—including some of the nation's most prominent newspaper columnists; the president of the University of California; Martin Luther King, Jr.; student protestors from various parts of the country; the chief justice of the

U.S. Supreme Court; and the Eisenhower brothers themselves. Some of these people made explicit reference to
Eisenhower's speech; others did not. The clever phrasing
of "military-industrial complex" and the Eisenhower imprimatur not only preserved earlier, related critiques of
militarism but also expanded into areas that neither Eisenhower nor his speechwriters could have imagined.

What follows are four detailed examples—outside the
context of Vietnam, and before the massive buildup of the
American presence there—in which the MIC was deemed
to be shaping public life in a malevolent way. They are, in
order: in shaping the nation's military budget and planning; in infringing upon civil liberties; in distorting national social and political priorities; and in affecting academic freedom, the role of universities, and the realm of
federal research.

"McNamara Has Been Conscious of the Problem"

One glaring question raised by Eisenhower's rhetoric is
the notion of immanence. Was the undue influence of the
military-industrial complex something to be feared but
still preventable? Or did it already exist, requiring good
citizens to identify and remove it? The latter view would
become widespread by the late 1960s. But well before

that, many believed the military-industrial complex was exerting a malign effect.

In two significant respects, the early days of the Kennedy administration could be seen as a vindication of Eisenhower's views. Although John Kennedy had campaigned for office advocating increased military spending, his administration learned within weeks of taking office that the much-hyped "missile gap" was a fiction. In an often blunt memoir, Kennedy's defense secretary Robert McNamara confirmed the view that Eisenhower and his aides commonly stated among themselves—that the Air Force's estimates of Soviet missile strength had been cooked. "It took my deputy, Roswell Gilpatric, and me no more than three weeks to learn that indeed there was a gap in offensive warheads," McNamara wrote. "However, as had been documented by the CIA, it was a gap very much in the favor of the United States. The Air Force, without any intention to deceive, had simply interpreted ambiguous data in ways that supported their weapons programs."[3]

Second, once in office, Kennedy felt a need to echo his predecessor's warning about the dangers of a powerful war machine. After two months in the White House, addressing a session of Congress devoted to the military budget, the new president insisted: "Neither our strategy nor our psychology as a nation—and certainly not our economy— must become dependent upon our . . . maintenance of a large military establishment. . . . Our arms must be subject to ultimate civilian control and command at all times."[4] Yet McNamara had reason to wonder whether civilian control was actually in place. Since the bombing of Hiroshima and Nagasaki, the leaders of the United States had pledged that the only proper role for nuclear weapons was to deter a nuclear attack. Kennedy, in his speech, affirmed: "Our arms will never be used to strike the first blow in any attack. . . . It is our national tradition." While that statement may have proven historically true, it did not, as both McNamara and Kennedy would soon learn, necessarily reflect what the military was actually planning.

As McNamara and his aides became familiar with the Defense Department, they uncovered factions within the military that believed in planning for a preemptive nuclear strike against the Soviet Union. "When I served in the Kennedy Administration, I learned that the capability to launch a first strike that would virtually eliminate Soviet nuclear forces was indeed the goal of some in the U.S. Air Force," McNamara wrote. "In a 1962 memorandum to the president, I quoted from an Air Force document: 'The Air Force has rather supported the development of forces which provide the United States a first-strike capability credible to the Soviet Union, as well as to our allies, by virtue of our ability to limit damage to the United States and our Allies to levels acceptable in the light of the circumstances and the alternatives available.'" Curtis LeMay, the commander of the Strategic Air Command and later vice chief of staff for the Air Force, is said to have told a group of civilian defense advisors in 1957 that if he learned via satellite that the Soviets were amassing their planes for a nuclear attack, "I'm going to knock the shit out of them before they take off the ground."[5]

Here, then, was a clear and startling instance in which the military establishment pursued a policy completely at odds with the stated position of the executive branch. Presumably McNamara could not have publicly revealed this at the time without creating a crisis. He set about trying to wean the Air Force off the weapons that he felt played into the first-strike capability planning—causing repeated clashes with defense contractors, the Joint Chiefs of Staff, and members of Congress whose districts benefited from military spending.[6] One such fight, over the RS-70 bomber, led to an outright constitutional challenge over whether Congress or the president has the ultimate authority to choose which weapons are built in the nation's name.[7] The RS-70 had begun life as the B-70 (the RS, for "reconnaissance and strike," was added later by the Air Force), and as a candidate Kennedy had supported its development in opposition to the Eisenhower administration, which had hoped to kill the program. It was designed to fly at very high altitude (like the U-2 spy plane) and at three times the speed of sound. When first conceived in the 1950s, this approach made military sense, but the development of effective Soviet anti-aircraft missiles toward the end of that decade led many to conclude that the bomber would be vulnerable to attack. Shortly after taking office, Kennedy submitted a military budget to Congress that substantially cut back plans for the B-70's production, and McNamara described the $10 billion plane as unnecessary to a nuclear strategy now more focused on intercontinental ballistic missiles.

This position infuriated LeMay, whom Kennedy had appointed chief of staff of the Air Force. LeMay's advocacy for the B-70 had some strategic justification. He feared overreliance on nuclear missiles—unlike manned bombers, they could not be recalled—and he did not think that the Air Force and Navy should be made to share a single bomber program, as McNamara and his efficiency-minded aides had proposed. But LeMay's lobbying also smacked of an institutional turf war, with the Air Force stubbornly clinging to recently acquired power.

Hoping to stave off the Air Force–congressional alliance that so vexed the Eisenhower White House, McNamara ordered LeMay not to testify before Congress about the B-70. Even so, for two years, Congress had appropriated money for the plane, which the administration simply declined to spend.

In 1962, this situation brought a showdown in Congress, led by Carl Vinson, the veteran chair of the House Armed Services Committee. On March 1 of that year, the committee unanimously dispensed $491 million for research and development of the B-70. It then took a further, apparently unprecedented step: it "ordered and directed" that the administration spend the money that had been allocated.

Many found it unsurprising that a congressional committee would act so ferociously to protect military spending. As author Nick Kotz has noted, twenty-one of the thirty-seven members of the committee represented districts where B-70 work was being conducted. The connections between military spending and the economy were beginning to be documented during this period. In January 1962, the newly created Arms Control and Disarmament Agency issued a report that, apparently for the first time, examined the economic impact of reducing military expenditure. The small volume, entitled *Economic*

Effects of Disarmament, noted a broad fear that disarmament could cause a depression; that "a sustained decline in defense expenditures could impair the long-term stability and growth of our economy"; and that certain industries, companies, and regions would face serious dislocation even if overall economic health could be preserved. It concluded that twenty-two states were highly dependent on military spending; in seven of them, more than 20 percent of all manufacturing jobs were directly tied to the military budget. "In some areas of the country the dependence on defense production is already very tangible and a serious source of concern. . . . certain states are clearly subject to disproportionately heavy impacts because of the relatively heavy dependence of their manufacturing on major items of procurement."[8] In Vinson's home state of Georgia, for example, Defense Department payrolls accounted for 6.8 percent of personal income, more than double the national average of 2.9 percent. And during the battle over the RS-70, the Pentagon and major companies that would build the plane—notably Boeing and North American Aircraft—let members of Congress know just how much spending was going to happen in their districts.

And thus the committee's action created a fascinating but divisive debate: Who is ultimately responsible for American military spending? While Congress's constitutional role is to provide funds, presumably the president's role as commander in chief gives the executive branch the final say in exactly how those funds are spent. Vinson's committee report said: "Let the test be made." Kennedy and Vinson were able to craft a compromise before the measure came to a full House floor vote, but some of the nation's most eminent journalistic observers saw the pernicious hand of the MIC at work. Marquis W. Childs of the *St. Louis Post-Dispatch*, who would go on to win the first Pulitzer Prize for commentary, wrote in a 1962 column of the power of an "invisible lobby" in the RS-70 showdown, and he declared: "Ever since General Eisenhower uttered his warning . . . about the threat of the domination of what he called the military-industrial complex the power of that complex has become more apparent." When the RS-70 came back before Congress a year later, James Reston in a *New York Times* column listed it with other clashes between the defense secretary and Congress, and he observed that the sustained attack on McNamara "seems to give some point to President Eisenhower's farewell address, in which he warned about the dangers of military and industrial forces combining to unbalance the nation." After quoting Eisenhower's speech, Reston added: "McNamara has been conscious of this danger ever since he entered the Pentagon but is more conscious of it now, especially when he sees political power on Capitol Hill added to the military-industrial complex."[9] This is an early, pivotal interpretation of what the MIC entails: distorting use of the military budget to build weapons for political purposes, regardless of whether they actually increase national security. And more strikingly than in any commentary immediately after Eisenhower's farewell, Congress is portrayed as a major player in perpetuating and strengthening the MIC.

Congress, of course, was never mentioned in the MIC section of Eisenhower's farewell speech, but Eisenhower knew full well the Pentagon's power to press its imperatives on elected officials. In a 1958 battle with Vinson and other congressional leaders over the reorganization of the Defense Department, Eisenhower reluctantly accepted a provision that allowed military personnel to go directly to Congress with any recommendations they felt appropriate, which the president labeled "legalized insubordination." And discussing his own thoughts behind his farewell speech in his 1965 memoir, Eisenhower noted: "Each community in which a manufacturing plant or a military installation is located profits from the money spent and the jobs created in the area. This fact, of course, constantly presses on the community's political representatives—congressmen, senators, and others—to maintain the facility at maximum strength."[10] What Eisenhower had not put into his own speech about Congress was, by the early 1960s, effectively placed there by others.

"Less Than a Full Citizen"

In 1962, Earl Warren delivered an unusually detailed address at New York University School of Law on the military and the Bill of Rights. Citing specifically Eisenhower's farewell address, the Supreme Court chief justice also struck an Eisenhowerian note of balance, arguing that while the military was a necessary institution in America, "the reach of its power must be carefully limited lest the delicate balance between freedom and order be upset. The maintenance of the balance is made more difficult by the fact that while the military serves the vital function of preserving the existence of the nation, it is, at the same time, the one element of government that exercises a type of authority not easily assimilated in a free society."[11]

Warren enumerated various ways in which the history of the Republic supported the notion of civilian control over the military, such as the separation of civilian and military judicial systems and the guarantee of fundamental constitutional rights of military personnel. Nonetheless, just as Eisenhower had, Warren recognized that there was a problem of scale. Democratic ideals (such as those defined in the Bill of Rights) conceived during an era when the United States had no standing army were not easily transferred to the era of America as a global superpower. "We cannot fail to recognize how our burgeoning army has posed difficult and unique problems for the Court in the application of constitutional principles," Warren said.

In Warren's view, there seemed little doubt that, at least on occasion, military imperatives had infringed on citizens' rights. One such instance was the denial of citizenship to any member of the military who had been convicted of desertion in a court martial; some seven thousand men in the Army alone were denationalized in this manner after World War II. Warren expressed the view (as indeed the Supreme Court had ruled in the 1958 *Trop v. Dulles* case) that stripping someone of his American citizenship constituted a cruel and unusual punishment and thereby violated the Eighth Amendment.

More disturbing were instances where arguments of national security had been used to strip civilians of their freedoms. Warren pointed specifically to the lawsuit *Hirabayashi vs. United States*, which challenged the curfews placed on Japanese Americans enacted by executive order from Franklin Roosevelt in 1942. The defendant in that case was a U.S.-born college student of Japanese descent. He had applied for and received conscientious objector status at the outbreak of World War II and, after Roosevelt's executive order went into effect, had declined to participate in the roundup of Asian Americans in Seattle. "I wanted to uphold the principles of the Constitution, and the curfew and evacuation orders which singled out a group on the basis of ethnicity violated them," Gordon Hirabayashi told one author. "It was not acceptable to me to be less than a full citizen in a white man's country."[12] He was arrested and spent ninety days in prison. When his lawsuit reached the Supreme Court in 1943, the justices voted 9–0 that his detention had not violated the Constitution. Similar cases were brought by Fred Korematsu in California and Minoru Yasui in Portland, Oregon, with the same results.

The Court's stated reason for ruling that the forced roundup and internment of tens of thousands of American citizens—into what were commonly labeled "concentration camps"—was constitutional was that military reasons justified it. Ethnic discrimination was legitimate, the justices ruled, because in wartime "residents having ethnic affiliations with an invading enemy may be a greater source of danger than those of a different ancestry."[13] Thus, the constitutional protection of citizens may be stripped by Congress and the executive branch, and, as long as the context is military necessity, there will be no judicial recourse. Or, as Warren put it in his speech, "There are some circumstances in which the Court will, in effect, conclude that it is simply not in a position to reject descriptions by the Executive of the degree of military necessity."

This concept of military override clearly troubled Warren, who had been attorney general of California during the internment and had supported it. He seemed to conclude that the role of the Court in such circumstances was actually separate from upholding the Constitution: "The fact that the Court rules in a case like *Hirabayashi* that a given program is constitutional, does not necessarily answer the question whether, in a broader sense, it actually is." This is a remarkable public admission from a Supreme Court justice, and it certainly would fit some people's definition of a garrison state—particularly given that a quarter of a century after Warren's speech, the Hirabayashi conviction was overturned on the grounds that the government withheld from the courts the fact that there was no military need for the president's executive order. Warren added that such circumstances were rare, particularly in peacetime, but noted that because of the enormous growth in the size and reach of the military, there were potential dangers stemming from the "influence exerted on the civil government by uniformed personnel and the suppliers of arms." It is clear, then, that the chief justice of the United States Supreme Court worried about the constitutional implications of the military-industrial complex, which is why he quoted that portion of Eisenhower's speech and exhorted his audience: "Coming from one who was our great Field Commander in World War II and for eight years Commander-in-Chief as President of the United States, these words should find lodgment in the mind of every American. It is also significant that both his predecessor and his successor have conveyed the same thought in slightly different words. I am sure that none of them thought for a moment that anyone was deliberately trying to change the relationship between the military and the civil government. But they realized, as we all must, that our freedoms must be protected not only against deliberate destruction but also against unwitting erosion."

The Revolving Door

"The most spectacular and important creation of the authoritarian and oligopolistic structure of economic decision-making in America is the institution called 'the military-industrial complex' by former President Eisenhower, the powerful congruence of interest and structure among military and business elites which affects so much of our development and destiny. Not only is ours the first generation to live with the possibility of world-wide cataclysm—it is the first to experience the actual social preparation for cataclysm, the general militarization of American society."[14]

So began a section of the Port Huron Statement, the sweeping manifesto issued by a few dozen young people in the name of Students for a Democratic Society during a Michigan convention in June 1962. It appears to be the earliest documented connection between Eisenhower's farewell speech and what was becoming known as the New Left (although portions of the "Old Left" also began using the term "military-industrial complex" at about this time).[15]

Here, the meaning of MIC, while attributed to Eisenhower, has effectively been filtered through C. Wright Mills, albeit with some significant additions. Tom Hayden, who had drafted the early versions of the Port Huron Statement, wrote his master's thesis at the University of Michigan on Mills, whom he later described as "the oracle of the New Left."[16] The Port Huron vision of the MIC held that it provided an economic and behavioral underpinning for the Marxist notion of a "false consciousness." That is, the Cold War and the American machinery necessary to win it, or at least perpetuate it, became a kind of socioeconomic glue that provided cohesion but blinded the population from seeing the martial state that was actually being constructed. Central to this idea were apathy and alienation. If, after all, the imperatives of business, military, and political elites were going to be fulfilled no matter what—whether in sustaining the Jim Crow South or in upholding colonialism (both significant concerns of the Port Huron Statement)—then what meaning could individual political participation hope to have? To combat this helplessness, SDS put a heavy emphasis on legislation, systems, and political theories that would empower individuals and encourage democratic participation, which would be an important trajectory in postwar American politics.

At first blush, such thinking appears far afield from anything that Eisenhower said or intended to say. And it is almost certain that the Port Huron Statement would have discussed these issues whether or not Eisenhower had ever uttered the phrase "military-industrial complex." Nonetheless, Eisenhower's imprimatur gives the idea credibility that it would probably not have had if associated only with a radical sociologist like Mills and some earnest left-wing students.

Moreover, the connection between the Port Huron State-

ment and the Eisenhower farewell speech is deeper than it
may appear. For one thing, the Port Huron Statement—
again, always using the lens of a Millsian elite class—is
quite explicit about the problem that would later be called
the revolving door, the ease with which top Pentagon officials became executives at military contractors and vice-
versa. "The intermingling of Big Military and Big Industry is evidenced in the 1,400 former officers working for
the 100 corporations who received nearly all the $21 bil-
lion spent in procurement by the Defense Department
in 1961," the statement asserted. "The overlap is most
poignantly clear in the case of General Dynamics, the
company which received the best 1961 contracts, employed the most retired officers (187), and is directed by a
former Secretary of the Army." Eisenhower's farewell
speech conspicuously does not mention, nor even allude
to, this problem. Yet the problem of a revolving door was
repeatedly discussed by both Malcolm Moos and Ralph
Williams from their very earliest conversations about what
Eisenhower's farewell speech should say. Thus, while the
Port Huron Statement attached the phrase "military-
industrial complex" to the concept of overlap between
contractors and military personnel, it did so in a way that
was consistent with what the Eisenhower White House
had been thinking.

Furthermore, Eisenhower's speech allowed for the notion that the MIC would have a "spiritual" impact on the American people and would affect the "very structure of our society."[17] Those are intrinsically subjective concepts, and sufficiently sweeping that the Mills–Hayden–Port Huron interpretation of them does not seem wholly unjustified. Neither was it unique; others concerned with America's spiritual direction also saw the MIC as an impediment. In a series of sermons written and delivered in the wake of the Montgomery bus boycott, beginning in 1955, Dr. Martin Luther King, Jr., began outlining his version of Gandhian nonviolence. One central issue that he tackled was the idea of nonconformism, that Christians, following Christ's example, must resist giving in completely to the dictates of any worldly society, be it the Roman Empire or modern America. King spoke repeatedly of the idea of the "mass mind" and the "rhythmic drumbeat of the status quo" as forces that thwarted contemporary Christians from being able to express their true moral views. Another such force was "jumboism"—the notion that we must all take refuge in big corporations, big cities, big buildings—which, he argued, made it difficult for people to view themselves as part of a minority, thus making it easier for injustice to prevail. "Not a few men, who cherish lofty and noble ideals, hide them under a bushel for fear of being called different," King said in a 1963 sermon. The segregation context was the most obvious: "Many sincere white people in the South privately oppose segregation and discrimination, but they are apprehensive lest they be publicly condemned." As was often the case, however, King saw in the immediate conflict of desegregation parallels to larger issues of international scope: "Millions of citizens are deeply disturbed that the military-industrial complex too often shapes national policy, but they do not want to be considered unpatriotic. Countless loyal Americans honestly feel that a world body such as the United Nations should include even Red China, but they fear being called Communist sympathizers."[18]

Here, then, the MIC is depicted as an instrument of quasi-authoritarian fear and coercion, which is not inconsistent with Eisenhower's oft-stated view of how a martial government might abuse its power. Indeed, in 1962, a year after his farewell speech, Eisenhower used the term "military-industrial complex" in the context of Napoleon and Robespierre (noting quickly that he had never met an American military officer who aspired to such power).[19]

"You Can't Even Passively Take Part!"

And so the idea of the MIC became for many a kind of standing populist receptacle for dissatisfaction with an economic and social order that seemed to value the collective over the individual, the automated over the manual, the views and goals of an elite over those that society democratically establishes for itself. This elastic interpretation of the MIC was well in place by the early 1960s, yielding some fairly exotic results. In December 1964, a Berkeley philosophy graduate student named Mario Savio returned to his hometown of New York City to give a press conference. He was a leader of several hundred students constituting the campus's "Free Speech Movement," who that fall had applied the tactics of the nation's burgeoning civil rights movement to disagreements between the Berkeley administration and many campus groups. Nine days earlier, Savio had delivered an impassioned, now-famous assault on the leadership of the University of California from the steps of Berkeley's Sproul Hall. "There's a time when the operation of the machine becomes so odious, makes you so sick at heart that you can't take part! You can't even passively take part! And you've got to put your bodies upon the gears and upon the wheels, upon the levers, upon all the apparatus—and you've got to make it stop! And you've got to indicate to the people who run it, to the people who own it—that unless you're free the machine will be prevented from working at all!"[20] He then introduced Joan Baez to the crowd, who sang "We Shall Overcome," and he led them into an occupation of the building, in which more than eight hundred were ultimately arrested.

Taking the SDS concept of anti-apathy a step further, Savio fused the rhetoric of civil disobedience with a plea for a kind of existential purity, a potent cocktail of protest at the time. The speech and the sentiment it represented were so influential that it is easy to draw a straight line between the Free Speech Movement and the anti-Vietnam movement, which many historians understandably do. But while Savio's speech was a tirade against bureaucracy and reactionaryism in various places—the university, government, labor unions, and the mainstream media—it never directly mentions the Army, Vietnam, or any of the related issues that within a few years would tear apart American campuses.[21] The New York press conference, however, while hammering similar themes, added a subtle, potent twist. Savio predicted that soon the protests on the Berkeley campus could well spread to other universities—including New York's Columbia University and New York University—because, he said, they had forfeited their commitment to scholarship and instead chosen to serve "the military-industrial complex."[22]

As with the above examples, the presumed malign influence of the military-industrial complex is not presented as an ominous future scenario: it is already here, and it has corrupted American universities. Another noteworthy aspect of Savio's comment is that the phrase "military-industrial complex" is now, not quite four years after Eisenhower's farewell speech, floating free of any reference to Eisenhower, which perhaps accounts for an application of the term that seems to have little to do with the military. Savio did not appear to feel it necessary to cite Eisenhower; neither did a *New York Times* reporter who covered the event.

But most remarkably, Savio's apparently radical assertion, knowingly or not, echoed an idea that had been expressed by his archnemesis: Clark Kerr, the president of the University of California. In his widely read book *The Uses of the University*, first published in 1963, a year before the Berkeley campus exploded on his watch, Kerr had written: "Intellect has also become an instrument of national purpose, a component part of the 'military-industrial complex.'"[23] While Savio's usage of the term MIC was bombastic, Kerr's was arguably even more extreme—how does one interpret the notion that intellect itself has been strapped to the MIC? While Savio wanted mostly to denounce this state of affairs, Kerr's book goes some way toward documenting it.

Certainly, during Eisenhower's administration, federal

grant money came to hold enormous sway over American universities. Higher education in 1960 received about $1.5 billion from the federal government—a hundredfold increase in twenty years, and accounting for 75 percent of all university expenditures on research. Moreover, nearly all of this money came from six federal agencies; in 1961, the Defense Department and Atomic Energy Commission accounted for 40 percent of the funds.[24]

Within the academy, this ballooning federal largesse was, through the early 1960s, usually viewed positively. It allowed scarce resources to be deployed on more traditional, student-serving activities, and it helped ensure that universities kept their research up to date. Some grumbled about the intrusive security clearances that national-security-related research required, and critics on the left have long maintained that such restrictions helped squelch radical ideas and suppress professors stretching back to the McCarthy period.[25] But, as Kerr's relatively complacent tone suggests, few within mainstream academia perceived that federal money was in and of itself a corrupting influence.

That situation would change, in no small part because universities were on the vanguard of U.S. involvement in Vietnam. It's hard to imagine a more thorough case of corrupting federal influence over universities than what occurred at Michigan State University (with, it should be said, the approval of the Eisenhower administration). MSU is a land-grant college whose longtime president John A. Hannah also served as assistant secretary of defense during Eisenhower's first term. Hannah, for one, had few qualms about melding the university's agenda with that of the military. "Our colleges and universities must be regarded as bastions of our defense, as essential to the preservation of our country and our way of life as supersonic bombers, nuclear-powered submarines and intercontinental ballistic missiles," he said in a 1961 speech.[26]

Beginning in 1955, MSU implemented a multimillion-dollar "nation-building" assistance program for the South Vietnamese government run by Ngo Dinh Diem.[27] University professors from the political science department, economics department, and College of Business—and a large contingent of advisors and support staff—provided technical assistance and training to Diem's police force, civil service, and public administration through a contract with a State Department agency called the International Cooperation Administration. In practical terms, the MSU professors were involved in delivering to Diem's palace guard such munitions as guns, ammunition, tear gas, trucks, and grenades. The relationship had begun with a direct phone call from Secretary of State John Foster Dulles to Hannah.[28] This began a long-term, personal relationship between Diem and MSU professor Wesley Fishel. (Although Fishel would later become disillusioned with Diem, he kept a keen interest in Vietnam and advised both the Kennedy and Johnson administrations.) Diem actually visited MSU's East Lansing campus on at least two occasions.

The project was rocky from the beginning, due in part to cultural differences between the Americans and Vietnamese, and to Diem's mercurial and dictatorial tendencies, which led to his downfall in the early 1960s. It was made more difficult by the fact that from the very beginning, the MSU team was expected to provide cover for the CIA in Vietnam; at least three people ostensibly working for MSU were in fact acting on behalf of American intelligence. Two of the program participants referred critically to its "somewhat forced hospitality as organizational cover for certain intelligence functions of the American government until mid-1959. Not only was the cover quite transparent, but what it did not conceal tended to bring the whole MSU endeavor under suspicion."[29]

Thus was a university used as an instrument of a secret foreign policy that almost certainly violated the 1954 Geneva Accord on Vietnam. Many historians have noted that the MSU experience not only propped up unrealistic assessments of America's role in Vietnam during the Eisenhower administration (and also provided some of the antics for the best-selling novel *The Ugly American*), but indeed created a kind of template for what would become America's disastrous military involvement. One writer called the MSU project "the most brazen interference by a university in the internal affairs of a foreign nation, [which] undoubtedly contributed to the full-scale war that later ensued under President Johnson."[30] The MSU program disbanded in 1962; a few years later, when the CIA's role in the MSU Vietnam assistance program was publicly revealed, it caused significant controversy on the MSU campus and well beyond. The notion that at least some universities had been compromised by the MIC was not a wild exaggeration.

"They Feared Reprisals"

It seems unlikely that Eisenhower—the onetime president of Columbia University—would have shared the view that the school's mission had been corrupted by the MIC. Yet Savio's and Kerr's concerns were very much in the spirit of Eisenhower's speech, in that they questioned whether government-funded research undermines academic independence.

Indeed, during this period, the retired Dwight Eisenhower and his younger brother Milton—who served as president of three universities, most notably in a long term at Johns Hopkins University—continued to express the fear that government aid was being used to control the direction of basic research and, more ominously, to muzzle critics who spoke out against government policies. Immediately after the November 1963 assassination of President Kennedy, newly sworn-in President Johnson requested a meeting with Eisenhower. Official minutes were taken of the issues discussed, but in a supplemental note in his own diary, Eisenhower said that he had expressed the following concerns to the new president: "I stated that throughout the country there has been uneasiness, if not fear, because of the tactics employed by the Justice Department and the IRS in the carrying out of their duties. Specifically, I said that I had heard some dismay expressed in business circles, in Universities, and even in Foundations, alleging a 'political party' type of questioning by IRS when supposedly engaged merely in examining financial accounts. Another allegation has been that if any corporation or University submitted before a Congressional Committee any testimony unfavorable to the Administration that the head of such an institution would be promptly warned by the Justice Department that any contracts between that institution and the Government would probably be cancelled."[31]

Eisenhower's allegations of government strong-arming are unfortunately as vague as they are disturbing. It seems likely, however, that at least some of the tales to which he alluded had come from his brother Milton. It was natural for the Eisenhower brothers to focus their attention on universities, given their university connections. Milton had established in the early 1960s an organization called the Republican Critical Issues Council, a kind of loosely organized think tank designed to promulgate centrist Republican positions (and, no doubt, to keep the aging Dwight in the spotlight). In a 1967 oral history interview, Milton was asked about the concept of the military-industrial complex, and after a historical discussion of the growth of the size of the military, he turned to some of the difficulties he'd faced trying to appoint advisors to this Republican-identified group:

> In setting up the space program, I wanted the vice-president of a leading American industrial enterprise to be the chairman. It happens that he was a PhD physicist, had managed great enterprise in the military establishment before he became the vice-president of the corporation. When I invited him to assume the chairmanship, he was quite friendly to the idea. But when he checked with his superiors and the board of

directors, they declined to permit him to accept, because they had a great many contracts with the federal government, and they feared reprisals. So he declined.

On the agricultural study, I asked a professor of a leading American university who universally would be recognized as one of the great agricultural authorities of this country. He checked with the president of his university, who became fearful because they were receiving many millions of dollars under hundreds of different grants from the federal government, and they feared reprisals.

Indeed, the newspaper at about this time carried the story of a professor at the University of Michigan who testified before a Senate committee in opposition to a federal activity, and the president of that university received a call from a person very high in the federal government which was (perhaps I should say) interpreted by the press as a threat to future grants to that university. . . . I think this is the—in actuality— the type of thing which [the president] feared when he made the farewell address, and warned against the military-industrial complex."[32]

Again, this is a remarkable assertion: the president's brother—who worked with him on the farewell address— is saying that in 1963 and 1964, the influence of the military-industrial complex was being asserted via censorious threats made by federal government agencies. Of course, with such spare details, it is difficult to verify or even con-

clusively identify the incidents to which Milton referred.
What can be verified is that, as President Eisenhower had
argued in his farewell address, "the prospect of domination of the nation's scholars by federal employment, project allocations, and the power of money is ever present."

SEVEN

In Full Fury

Early in 1966 the world seemed pretty bright to the managers of Dow Chemical. The company, based in Midland, Michigan, was the largest manufacturer of industrial and consumer plastics in the United States, and the growth of plastic was explosive; Dow was making more than a billion pounds of the stuff a year. Whether American housewives preferred Saran Wrap (first sold for home use in 1953) or Handi-Wrap (first sold in 1963), their money went into Dow's coffers. In 1965, Dow was one of only a few dozen American companies to surpass a billion dollars in annual revenue, and it was throwing off profit at three times the rate of a decade earlier. First-quarter profits in 1966 were up 32.2 percent over the year before, and Dow, which already employed some thirty thousand people around the world, was still expanding. In February 1966 the company announced a $14.5 million expansion of its chemical manufacturing facilities in Louisiana and said it was considering opening a "multimillion dollar" manganese processing plant in Ogden, Utah—right near Hill Air Force Base.

That location was not entirely coincidental. Popular or not, the escalating American military involvement in Vietnam was good for business. In early 1966 Dow, along with United Technology in Connecticut, had received an Air Force contract to manufacture 75,000 tons of Napalm-B, a newly tweaked version of an incendiary jelly used to rain fire on the North Vietnamese landscape when the United States began bombing there in 1965. (Some 400,000 tons of napalm would be used over the course of that war.) The napalm contract quickly turned into a public relations fiasco. Reports of napalm use in Vietnam had become routine in the mainstream press, but activist publications (notably the monthly magazine *Ramparts*) had carried especially graphic accounts and presented high estimates of civilian casualties. In April, protestors in Redwood City, California, were able to put on the ballot an initiative denying use of city property for the manufacture of napalm. Four women were arrested trying to block shipments of napalm out of a Dow facility in San Jose. Pickets began springing up outside Dow's offices in Manhattan's Rockefeller Center, with protestors carrying signs that read "Napalm Burns Babies, Dow Makes Money." Protests spread to dozens of universities, turning Dow's recruitment efforts into occasionally nightmarish episodes. An October 1967 trip to Harvard University—where napalm had been invented during World War II—led to a Dow recruiter being detained for seven hours in a chemistry lab room.[1]

In a short time, Dow—not an especially large military contractor—had become the poster child for corporate complicity with an increasingly unpopular war. A historian of the company has called the targeting of Dow "perhaps the most abusive attack ever launched against an American business firm." At the end of 1966, a Dow executive mused, "I would hate for Dow to come out of Viet Nam with the 'Merchants of Death' label that was pinned on du Pont after the first World War; and yet, unless we come to grips with this problem, it is likely to happen."[2]

This is what, for many, the military-industrial complex had come to mean: that industry was synonymous with militarism, that industry supported the military, and that to work for or buy from industry was to be complicit in an unjust war. It was one of many interpretations of the MIC making up the antiwar zeitgeist. By the late 1960s the MIC had become a loosely connected intellectual federation, itself a virtual complex, elaborating core ideas until they expanded into provocative, often explosive theories. Like the Port Huron Statement, the MIC was a political cause, a rallying point for the left, for whom it explained a seemingly pointless war. Whereas the tone of earlier treatments was ominous, prophetic, and descriptive, the MIC in the Vietnam era was often the target of furious rhetoric as well as increasingly specialized investigation. The expansion of the MIC thesis during this period included a deeper focus on the specific actions of Congress, lobbyists, and other players in the military budget process; an elaboration of the overall economic effects of the MIC (not surprisingly, they were usually found to be negative) leading to theories that the Pentagon and its contractors were "converging" into a single entity; and increased attention, especially on the part of protest groups, to the connections between the military and civilian economies.

The Rise of William Proxmire

Given the leading role that the legislative branch plays in the MIC, it is ironic that one of the most important apostles of the anti-MIC church was himself a legislator. William Proxmire was first elected to the U.S. Senate from

Wisconsin in 1957, to the seat once held by Joseph Mc-Carthy. From the start the onetime Wall Streeter focused on economic matters—such as antitrust policy, interest rates, and the fate of small businesses—which at times made him a vocal critic of his fellow Democrats John Kennedy and Lyndon Johnson. In early 1965, during the early stages of the troop buildup in Vietnam, Proxmire supported the Johnson administration's policies of attempting to coordinate negotiations between Communist and anti-Communist forces there. But by 1966, he counted himself among the "doves" who opposed further escalation of American involvement.

These twin concerns of economic policy and the war became joined, and Proxmire became a fervent advocate of lower taxes and reduced government spending, especially military spending. He was not immune to the lure of federal money: he supported defense appropriations that boosted the shipbuilding industry in Wisconsin, as well as milk price supports that benefited the state's dairy farms. But as he and his staff burrowed into the military budget, they dredged up instance after instance of waste and mismanagement. In late 1967, he announced that a General Accounting Office report he had commissioned discovered "shocking abuse" of $15 billion of government-owned tools and facilities which, he said, were being used without payment by private military contractors for their own purposes. In a January 1968 press conference, he named twenty-three military contractors who he said had engaged in this misuse, including Boeing, Raytheon, Sikorsky Aircraft, Bendix, TRW, and, curiously, two universities. This landed Proxmire on the front page of the *New York Times*, with a signature quotation: "I think this is an excellent example of the military industrial complex at work, with the victim being . . . the taxpayer."[3]

The specific context of this charge was not actually the Vietnam War. Nearly all the cases cited by the GAO report involved contracts dating from the early 1960s, and many of the big-ticket items were for use of land or facilities (such as airport hangars located in the United States). In addition, some of the violations were technical; the commercial use of public equipment was not itself illegal, but it required prior Defense Department approval that had not been sought. Still, Proxmire had found his cause. More than any other person, he would come to embody the interpretation of the MIC as a bureaucracy that spends without accountability and perpetuates waste as part of its profit making. It became a crusade; over the next few years, committees he controlled held hearings on military contracting, Pentagon management, contractor profits, and every manner of procurement issues. A crucial 1969 report issued by Proxmire's Joint Economic Committee of the Congress, called *The Economics of Military Procurement*, became a kind of bible for critics of the MIC. He would expand on its themes in a 1970 book called *Report from Wasteland: America's Military-Industrial Complex*. Given that he was by that time a committed opponent of the Vietnam War—an issue that had split the national Democratic Party—his attacks on the MIC were inevitably interpreted as opposing the Vietnam War by proxy.

Proxmire's goal was at least as much to galvanize Congress as to get America out of Vietnam. For all the fault his congressional hearings found with the Pentagon and its contractors—cost overruns, price collusion, regulatory capture, inefficiency, misstatements of enemy capability, lack of accountability—Proxmire clearly recognized that Congress was writing the checks. He was especially well placed to spotlight the lopsided power held by committee chairmen; the contractors' arm-twisting of local officials that ended up as pleas to federal legislators to support weapons contracts, regardless of whether the system at hand was militarily necessary; and the routine approval of military budget requests without substantive review. He summed it all up with the observation that Congress was a "pushover for the Pentagon."[4]

In later years, scholars and advocates would continue to develop the path that Proxmire blazed, analyzing Congress's role in the MIC at an atomic or even subatomic level of detail. For example, a 1972 paper by Arnold Kanter, covering the years 1960 to 1970, argued that despite all the attention drawn by showdowns between Congress and Presidents Eisenhower and Kennedy, the difference in defense budgets between what the executive branch requested and what the legislature approved was statistically quite small. Kanter, who would later hold high positions in the State Department, further argued that Congress rarely made major changes in two important defense budget areas—personnel, and operations and maintenance—concentrating its efforts instead on procurement and R&D. He also noted that when international tensions are high, the difference between the executive request and congressional appropriation was near zero. Although it was not his intention, his finding could be read as an incentive for the MIC to heighten tensions or even start wars.

The depth of analysis around military procurement issues beginning in the 1970s could almost justify an academic program in "MIC Studies." In subsequent years, analysts would examine nearly every conceivable aspect of Congress's relationship to military budgets, including political party affiliation, geographic distribution, committee membership and committee leadership, electoral outcomes, the timing of elections, and the role of subcontractors.[5]

Institutionalized Anger

What is striking about the Vietnam-era version of the MIC critique is how vehement its rhetoric could be. Eisenhower in his farewell address had struck a tone of grave concern, calling attention to an issue so that an enlightened citizenry might prevent dire occurrences. His longtime correspondent Norman Cousins continued, through his work with the Committee for a SANE Nuclear Policy, to fight within the system to achieve concrete goals such as arms reduction and test ban treaties. But to the most vociferous critics, such efforts seemed futile; the very project of America was inextricably bound up in military excess. By the end of the decade, the MIC had acquired such ominous synonyms as the "warfare state" and the "national security state." An economist who worked on Proxmire's committee wrote in 1969: "Only recently has research started to hang some real meat on [Eisenhower's] bony, provocative phrase, 'military-industrial complex.' What is emerging is a real Frankenstein's monster. Not only is there considerable evidence that excessive military spending has contributed to a misallocation of national resources, but the conclusion seems inescapable that society has already suffered irreparable harm from the pressures and distortions thus created."[6] That same year, Richard J. Barnet, who had worked in the Kennedy administration, published a book on the MIC called *The Economy of Death*. Another critical book, *The Pentagon Watchers*, asserted: "It is perhaps ironic that America, whose leaders claim that they have only responded to the world-wide challenge of totalitarian regimes in Russia and China, should increasingly resemble the repressive state that George Orwell depicted in *1984*. As in that work, the life of the state has become an end in itself, and as in Fascist Italy or Nazi Germany, the work of the state becomes the making of war."[7]

Those two books represent another significant milestone in MIC thinking—namely, its institutionalization. Both were products of the Institute for Policy Studies, which Barnet and Marcus Raskin had founded in 1963. Both men were disaffected government analysts who'd worked in the State and Defense Departments. The Brookings Institution, a far less radical outfit (Robert S. McNamara sat on its board of trustees), also trained its eye on military procurement issues. An influential 1968 Brookings report called *Government Contracting and Technological Change*, looking broadly and historically at the issues raised by contracting throughout government, largely confirmed Proxmire's view of the Pentagon as an unchecked source of wasteful spending. It determined that many big military contracts in the 1950s "ultimately involved costs in excess of original contractual estimates of from 300 to 700 per cent."

Another institution that sprang up in 1969 was National Action/Research on the Military-Industrial Complex, a project of the American Friends Service Committee in Philadelphia. The project was a clearinghouse for information on the military, business, and universities that eventually produced its own pamphlets and videos. Its research was also instrumental in an early project of the Council on Economic Priorities, a think tank founded in 1969 in Washington, DC, by a young former stockbroker named Alice Tepper. Over the following decades the council—often with funding from labor unions, the Carnegie Corporation, and the Ottinger Foundation, among others—would publish a number of books on different aspects of the MIC: *Military Maneuvers: An Analysis of the Interchange of Personnel between Defense Contractors and the Department of Defense* (1975); *B-1 Bomber: An Analysis of Its Strategic Utility, Cost, Constituency and Economic Impact* (1976); *Iron Triangle: The Politics of Defense Contracting* (1981); *Military Expansion, Economic Decline*

(1983). Yet it was a CEP book published in the fall of 1970, *Efficiency in Death*, that in many ways crystallized thinking about the MIC and gave it a lasting impact. Produced with research from the American Friends Service Committee, *Efficiency in Death* focused exclusively on the manufacture of antipersonnel weapons, primarily cluster bombs, which were designed to kill human beings as opposed to destroying property and military installations. After some introductory description, the book consists almost entirely of information about the hundred largest private companies involved in the manufacture of these weapons. A few of the larger firms, such as Honeywell and Sperry-Rand, were well-known general military contractors. But many were familiar manufacturers of everyday products: among others, the Bulova Watch Company, General Motors, Motorola, Rubbermaid, Uniroyal, and Whirlpool.[8] Nearly all the data was presented with the dispassion of a Wall Street analyst's company report, yet the implication was clear: invest in, work for, or patronize these companies, and you are complicit in the horrible, burning deaths of civilians in Vietnam. What Tepper and her colleagues were doing with the MIC went much further than the time-honored boycott; they were suggesting that the tools of activism could be melded to the tools of investing to make participation in war unattractive from the point of view of corporate finance. This was the beginning of what would become known as socially responsible investing.

Conversion or Convergence?

Just as a new generation of activists was delving into the minutiae of how corporations aided the war effort, so too was a new set of economists trying to make sense of the economic impact of armament and disarmament. Central to this effort was the work of Seymour Melman, an economist at Columbia University. Melman, one of the founders of SANE along with Norman Cousins, devoted a half century to exploring the intersections between the economy and the military. As early as 1962, he had edited a volume of essays called *Disarmament: Its Politics and Economics*, in which a number of contributors (including Bertrand Russell) laid out plans for inspection regimes, industrial conversion, the role of the United Nations, and the risk of nuclear proliferation in the wake of superpower disarmament. Through the late 1960s, the bulk of his published work was devoted to programmatic examinations of how to convert the MIC into a peace economy.[9] He also tried to draw attention to the substantial opportunity costs of a vast military sector. In a 1965 book he wrote: "The long-drawn-out Cold War has diverted high-grade talent from civilian work. One man cannot at the same time be a designer of merchant ships and a researcher on rocket airframes. By favoring rockets we have automatically chosen guns rather than butter."[10]

That formulation at least implied an economy that could be reversed through disarmament. But Vietnam made Melman substantially more pessimistic. In his landmark 1970 book *Pentagon Capitalism*, Melman depicted the American state as fully captured by the necessity of managing its war-based economy, a result of what he labeled "an institutionalized power-lust." Eisenhower, according to Melman, had correctly described the loose federation of powerful forces that made up the MIC. But in the intervening decade, centralization and aggrandizement of power in the Defense Department had introduced a formal structure to the MIC that was destined to destroy the American economy. It was not enough to think of America's actions in Vietnam as a form of imperialism; for Melman, there was "now added an institutional network that is parasitic at home. This combination is the new imperialism."[11]

Of the theorists working on military-economic issues in the late 1960s and 1970s, Murray L. Weidenbaum is something of a standout figure. Alone among the key writers on the subject, he held prominent positions within a military contracting firm (he was chief economist at Boeing from 1958 to 1963) and within two Republican administrations (Nixon and Reagan). He has made some effort to disassociate himself from the MIC—which, if anything, makes his criticisms of the MIC more credible. Since the mid-1960s, Weidenbaum argued that by working for the Pentagon, military contractors may harm themselves in several ways. They create disincentives to develop as commercial firms; they lose the incentive and ability to innovate; and they make themselves less attractive to investors, even though they may be more profitable than comparably sized civilian firms. Weidenbaum could be considered a free-market critic of the MIC.

As such, when he described in an influential 1968 paper a growing "convergence" between the Department of Defense and its major suppliers, Weidenbaum was cautioning against it—not because he thought the relationship was wasteful or damaging to the U.S. economy, or because it ill-served the nation's needs, but because the suppliers were damaging their own long-term growth prospects by allowing themselves to become dependent on government funding.[12] This perspective may have reflected his experience at Boeing. Intriguingly, in his "convergence" paper he wrote: "The major exception to this lack of entrepreneurship and willingness to bear risks in commercial markets is the Boeing Company, which has not won a major military competition since 1958. During the past decade, that company has invested several hundred million dollars of its own funds in commercial aircraft development, with considerable success."

Another way of looking at convergence is: Why not cut out the middleman? Two entities—a contracting Pentagon and a class of contractor companies—could be merged into one. The government could simply own the major contractors outright, and presumably the removal of the profit requirement would save money for the taxpayer. This position was most associated with John Kenneth Galbraith, who had argued that Big Business and Big Government generally were on this path: "Increasingly it will be recognized that the mature corporation, as it develops, becomes part of the larger administrative complex associated with the state. In time the line between the two will disappear."[13] In congressional testimony and in a 1969 essay, Galbraith suggested that military contractors be treated as public entities.[14]

There are several rejoinders to this argument, most obviously that permanent nationalization of large corporations has little precedent in U.S. history, in part because many doubt that government-run manufacturers could really be more innovative and efficient than private ones.[15]

But a more tantalizing response is that, without explicitly articulating a policy of nationalization, the U.S. government in the 1960s and 1970s actually did enter into the business of propping up—in some cases outright owning—some of the companies that supplied the Pentagon.

The best-known instance was Lockheed Aircraft, at the time the country's largest military contractor, which began to struggle in the late 1960s despite a hefty $1.9 billion contract secured in the middle of the decade to build the C-5A military transport plane. Lockheed posted losses of $19.5 million in 1969 and $86.3 million in 1970. Crippled by cost overruns and teetering on the edge of bankruptcy, it petitioned the Defense Department for an unprecedented $600 million in federal loan guarantees. In the summer of 1971, Congress authorized the government to guarantee up to $250 million in loans; the bill passed the Senate only with a tie-breaking vote cast by Vice President Spiro Agnew. This episode prompted Proxmire to coin the term "corporate welfare."

While the Lockheed bailout was the largest and best-known instance of direct government intervention to save a military contractor, subsequent journalistic investigations turned up numerous, previously unrevealed (and now largely forgotten) episodes in which the military acted to save companies that supplied it. In 1972, a small penny-stock company on Long Island called GAP Instrument Corporation found itself unable to fulfill a $3.1 million contract to build fire-control consoles for Navy destroyers. The company wanted to renegotiate the contract at a higher price, but the Navy refused; the Navy also considered a loan, but concluded that it would simply saddle GAP with debt that it would be unable to pay. So the Navy, invoking an obscure provision of the War Powers Act, bought all GAP's preferred shares for $1.7 million and became its largest shareholder.

This deal, while small, was nonetheless indefensible by any conventional free-market theory. The company had lost money for four years running and was effectively insolvent. Its common stock was trading for the smallest amount then possible, 12.5 cents per share, giving the entire company, charitably, a market value of $200,000. In addition, the preferred shares had no resale value. The best rationale that a Defense Department official could offer was sheer desperation: "It is a last gasp. When a guy comes before you in this case, he is damn near bankrupt, and we're saying the sheriff is standing there with a padlock. We would have closed his doors unless he got some relief."[16] *Time* magazine viewed this development squarely in the context of Eisenhower's farewell, quipping that "the hyphen that separates the military-industrial complex . . . may have grown one notch shorter."[17]

Increasing Intimacy

The notion that the Pentagon could be the majority owner of a private business was in some ways unsurprising. One major trend in MIC thinking in the late 1960s was to analyze the military's encroachment on what was perceived as civilian territory. This critique was partly a natural extension of other Vietnam-era protests, notably resistance to the draft and efforts to remove the Reserve Officer Training Corps from college campuses. Universities were often the crossroads where military and civilian influence intersected; as noted in the previous chapter, as early as 1963 Berkeley president Clark Kerr had observed that intellect had become a component of the MIC. In May 1967, *Phi Delta Kappan*, a magazine for educators, devoted a special issue to "the increasing intimacy" of civilian and military educational efforts. The magazine noted that this intimacy provided benefits, but also remarked that "the problems it raises range from baffling to frightening."[18] The academy and the military were bound to cooperate on some level because "national security is at once a military problem and a philosophical, psychological, political and educational problem." At the same time, the article went on, the two institutions were also bound to compete: for manpower, for resources, and for how young Americans think.

That competition was now an open conflict. In September 1966, twenty-two American scientists, including seven Nobel Prize winners, signed a petition urging the U.S. government to stop using chemical and biological weapons, and this issue soon exploded on university campuses where military-funded research on herbicides, tear gas, bacterial agents, and other weapons was going on. In early 1967, the trustees of the University of Pennsylvania—under pressure from students and faculty—rejected two million-dollar Defense Department contracts to study biological and chemical warfare. This decision was reached partly because of the direct connection to Vietnam and partly because many professors believed that classified research—regardless of who paid for it—was inimical to the spirit of intellectual inquiry. Within months, similar debates erupted at Stanford, MIT, and elsewhere.[19]

Some on college campuses defended military research, classified or otherwise, as necessary to keep faculty at the cutting edge of their fields.[20] Few, however, would publicly defend another government activity on college campuses: the CIA's secret funding of the National Student

Association. Dating back to the 1950s, the CIA spent millions of dollars to turn the NSA into a front group, used to influence student opinion and gather intelligence on student leaders at home and abroad. That infiltration dovetailed with the FBI's domestic spying and dirty tricks under COINTELPRO, whereby disinformation was circulated to discredit and divide American radical groups, including the Black Panthers and the American Indian Movement.[21] It is debatable whether such activities actually represent part of the MIC. But for many, the Cold War rationalizations for domestic spying, and its consistent use to target nonviolent political dissent, constituted an arm of the garrison state.

The influence of the Pentagon extended well beyond the university. In the late 1960s, Senator J. William Fulbright—a very early opponent of the Vietnam War—began a series of hearings and speeches in which he showed how the military was trying to mold public opinion at home and abroad. Tactics such as briefings and press releases were by this time quaintly outdated. The modern military, in Fulbright's view, was a five-star public relations machine with tens of millions of dollars at its disposal. It organized fact-finding missions to win over community leaders who might oppose military installments near their homes; it dispatched thousands of speakers every month to local Rotary clubs and USO councils; it acted as a literary agency for pro-Pentagon magazine articles written by members of the military; it deployed five television camera crews to depict U.S. actions in Vietnam in a positive light; it targeted interviews with soldiers to their hometown newspapers and radio stations; and it lent out ships, planes, and other materials to cinematic projects (such as *The Green Berets*) in return for guarantees that the films would be in the "best interest" of the Defense Department. Fulbright warned that these activities were part of a creeping militarism that could allow the MIC "to acquire power comparable to that of the German General Staff in the years before World War I."[22]

The Honeywell Project

But criticisms of the Pentagon's abstract power were often simply the backdrop to more direct action. Across America, on college campuses and off, through church groups and ad hoc activist organizations, Americans were physically opposing what they saw as the MIC, directing action at corporations with occasionally violent tactics. These actions—not always over Vietnam—made the early Dow Chemical protests look modest. Over a few weeks in April 1970, the annual shareholders' meetings of nine major corporations, including Boeing and Gulf Oil, were attacked. One particularly visible group was the Honeywell Project, a coalition of Minnesota activists who opposed Honeywell's production of cluster bombs. As a military-linked firm, Honeywell was a much larger and more logical target than Dow; it was the largest private employer in Minnesota and the sixteenth-largest Pentagon contractor. The protestors argued that because cluster bombs were designed specifically to kill people, their use constituted a war crime under the post–World War II Nuremberg Principles.

Led by Marv Davidov, an Army veteran who had participated in the Freedom Ride civil rights protest, the Honeywell Project targeted all facets of the company. It met with board members, leafleted the cluster bomb factory in Hopkins, Minnesota, and bought shares of Honeywell stock, which in 1970 it used to bring thousands of protestors to the company's annual shareholder meeting in Minneapolis.[23] The resulting mayhem caused the meeting to be cut short after fourteen minutes. Hundreds of protestors, locked outside the company headquarters, began throwing bottles at the building. Scores of Minneapolis policemen were called in and sprayed the crowd with Mace.

Two days later, the Nixon administration announced that the U.S. military had invaded Cambodia, igniting further protests across the country. In Kent State, Ohio, four students were shot to death by National Guard troops. The Honeywell Project protestors—many of whom had affiliations with the University of Minnesota—took their demonstrations to the Minneapolis campus. On May 4, five thousand students and faculty members voted for a university-wide strike to protest the Cambodia invasion. The action threatened to turn ugly when hundreds of students began to occupy Morrill Hall, and the university president decided to speak to the crowd. He proposed a one-day teach-in, but the demonstrations continued. On May 16, the protestors again confronted the university's president with five demands, including the removal of ROTC from campus, an end to war-related research, and the divesting of university stock in companies providing munitions. Once again, the university president was able to stave off violence through personal interaction with the protestors.

The university president was Malcolm Moos. If the protestors had any awareness that Moos had introduced the term "military-industrial complex" to the world, it has left scant historical trace.

EIGHT

"Eisenhower Must Be Rolling Over in His Grave"

"From the White House and the office of the president of the United States, we present an address by Dwight D. Eisenhower. This is the farewell address for President Eisenhower, whose eight years as chief executive come to an end at noon Friday." With this television introduction begins the 2005 feature-length documentary *Why We Fight*, which marks something of a renaissance for Eisenhower's farewell. From the late 1980s through the early part of the twenty-first century, discussions of the MIC went relatively quiet. The few pieces of critical analysis of the MIC published after the 1980s have broken little conceptual ground; rather, the strands of the argument as they stood at the end of the Vietnam War have continued to spin out. But recently, the prolonged wars in Iraq and, to a lesser extent, in Afghanistan have renewed interest in the MIC. *Why We Fight*, directed by Eugene Jarecki and focused on the American addiction to a permanent war economy, is the most elaborate popular expression of the notion that a military-industrial complex was largely responsible for the Iraq war that began in 2003. The film points to military contractors' need to innovate and show off their products in order to keep contracts coming, the importance of oil for national security, and particularly the connections between military infrastructure provider Halliburton and Vice President Dick Cheney. Following a thorough discussion of Eisenhower's speech—including interviews with Eisenhower's son John and granddaughter Susan—one commentator says: "I would think Eisenhower must be rolling over in his grave."

Specific conflicts raised by the Iraq War have revived interest in the MIC: the role of Cheney and Halliburton; the controversial detention center in Guantanamo Bay; the torture revealed in the Abu Ghraib prison; the privatization of security and combat as represented by the Blackwater firm; and the overruns in cost, length of engagement, and American lives. There are other indications, too, of a renewed fascination with Eisenhower's farewell. By early 2010, video versions of the address had been viewed more than half a million times on YouTube. And few presidential phrases have been more honored linguistically. The suffix "-industrial complex" has become a convenient (and certainly overused) way to describe the meshing of public and private interests, usually in a manner suggesting that profit motivations have trumped rational policy assessments. Critics of the dramatic expansion of the United States penal system often refer to the "prison-industrial complex."[1] Financial author Barry Ritholtz dubbed the high-risk housing bubble market of the early twenty-first century a "real estate–industrial complex."[2] Global warming deniers speak of a "climate-industrial complex." One reads of a pharmaceutical-industrial complex, a medical-industrial complex, even an "organic-industrial complex" of mass-produced food marketed as healthy. While these supposed complexes are usually thought to stand on their own, some energetic observers want to tie them all back to the original. A 2008 book by Nick Turse carried the tongue-in-cheek title *The Complex: Mapping America's Military-Industrial-Technological-Entertainment-Academic-Media-Corporate Matrix.*

Does a renewed interest in the MIC mean that it still exists, fifty years after Eisenhower's speech, and still exerts unwarranted influence? An obvious yardstick for answering this question—and one of Eisenhower's chief concerns—is overall military spending. Since the early 1950s, anyone who has expected American military spending to shrink significantly in absolute terms has nearly always been disappointed. Many commentators have concluded that America's military and political elite have exaggerated or even manufactured threats to national security so as to maintain high levels of military spending.[3] While such theories can veer into conspiracy, they were not unknown in the Eisenhower White House. At any rate, the spending numbers speak for themselves. Robert Higgs has calculated that in the period from 1948 to 1989, real military spending in 2005 dollars came to an amount just shy of $13 trillion. The overall trend during this period was for military spending to rise every year, a trend that holds true more or less independently of any assessment of increased threats to national security.[4] Simply put, the fact of the United States being relatively at peace has little impact on how much it spends on its military—which strongly suggests that other forces are at work.

Hence, a series of would-be military slowdowns have been announced but have never actually materialized. In the late 1960s, when Richard Nixon began to talk about ending America's involvement in Vietnam, economists and policymakers prepared for a demilitarization that never happened. When the Cold War ended, many political leaders touted the idea of a "peace dividend," money once devoted to defending against the USSR that could be used for other purposes. During the 1992 presidential campaign, for example, candidates from both parties projected cutting between $66 billion and $200 billion over five years from future military spending.[5] Adjusted for inflation, some reductions did occur in the 1990s, but they were reversed during the George W. Bush administration. Military spending under Obama (taking into account not only the budget line for the Defense Department but also interest on military-related debt, spending on Iraq and Afghanistan, military spending from other departments, and veterans' benefits) is now more than a trillion dollars a year, significantly higher in constant dollars than during the Cold War period, the Vietnam War, or the Reagan-era buildup. And this is in the absence of any comparable enemy investment; the United States spends more on its military than all other nations combined.

Of course, absolute military expenditure is not the only, or necessarily best, yardstick. Eisenhower's concern was that the military would grow out of proportion to the nation as a whole. Thus an instructive (if not quite definitive) measure of the size of the military budget is to compare it to other government expenditures and the overall economy. In most instances these ratios are dramatically lower than they were in 1961. During the Korean War, military expenditures took up some 70 percent of all government spending; when Eisenhower delivered his farewell, the number was closer to 50 percent. Today, by most reckoning, it is about 20 percent, although some economists maintain that using a more realistic definition of federal spending yields a much higher percentage being spent for military purposes.[6] Alex Roland has suggested another yardstick that speaks to Eisenhower's original observation: total military research and development as a percentage of government spending. This number shoots up dramatically from the end of the Korean War until the mid-1960s—from about 2 percent to about 12 percent—a growth that may explain Eisenhower's urgency around the issue of a scientific-technological elite. It has since declined and is today around 5 percent.[7]

Another common method of measuring the military's influence is to compare military spending to the overall American economy. Like all yardsticks, this one has its limitations, but it gets to the heart of the issue of a permanent war economy. Since Eisenhower left office in 1961, the gross domestic product of the United States, measured in constant 2005 dollars, has gone from about $2.9 trillion to about $13.3 trillion in 2008, more than a fourfold increase.[8] Although some economists and others have maintained that a vibrant military sector is a sine qua non for the growth of the American economy, the relationship between military spending and economic growth is not linear, and it is nearly impossible to predict economic activity based on the level of military spending. Since the end of the Korean War, the broad trend for military spending as a percentage of GDP has been downward, from about 12.5 percent when Eisenhower left office to about 7.3 percent in 2008. During that half century, this percentage has seen a steady decline with few (and fairly modest) periods of relative military expansion. Two of these have been well explored by historians and economists: the Vietnam War and the Reagan military buildup. Less well analyzed is that we are living through another such period in the early twenty-first century. As the accompanying graph shows, military spending relative to the overall economy hit a post–World War II low of 6 percent in 2001. Since then it has increased every year and now stands at more than 7 percent, near where it was in the late 1970s, when the Cold War was still in effect.[9]

This rise is perhaps not surprising, given increased security spending in the wake of the 9/11 attacks and the costs of fighting wars in Iraq and Afghanistan. But during this period the United States also experienced an

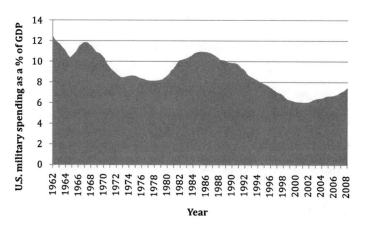

U.S. military spending as a percentage of GDP, 1962–2008.

economic contraction which, by some measures, was the most severe since the Great Depression. A deep recession also occurred in the early 1980s, another period when military spending began to expand. If military spending is a form of economic stimulus, then, it is not a very effective one, and the long and arbitrary lag time between outlays and growth would seem to render it useless to policymakers.

However, if we think of the relationship between military spending and the economy as a fraction, these figures say at least as much about the denominator as they do about the numerator. The real story these numbers tell is the stunning postwar expansion of the American economy, a butterfly that has largely broken free of the military cocoon spun during World War II and the Korean War. Moreover, a significant portion of that growth is attributable to the commercialization of technologies— including digital computers, microchips, satellites and telecommunications, aeronautics, computer networking, and the Internet—that were once under military control. So while it is possible that today's level of American military spending might inspire Eisenhower to roll over in his grave, he might barely recognize in today's America the "industrial" half of his formulation. Our economy and society have a vastly different relationship to the military than when Eisenhower left office. In some ways, the very term "military-industrial" is outdated, given that America has for decades been deindustrializing. American manufacturing employment peaked in 1979 at approximately 19.5 million jobs. By mid-2009 it had dipped below 12 million jobs and is unlikely ever to return to 1970s levels. Manufacturing now makes up less than 9 percent of all American jobs, the lowest percentage since the Bureau of Labor Statistics began keeping figures in 1939.

The military has also declined as an employer, in both relative and absolute terms. Eisenhower gave his speech during a time when huge percentages of Americans had personally served in the military, many involuntarily; he noted that "three and a half million men and women are directly engaged in the defense establishment." Direct military employment increased during the Vietnam period, and the Department of Defense says today that it employs about 3 million people and is the largest employer in the United States. But again, the denominator is different—the United States has about 125 million more people than it did in 1961. Equally important is the end of the draft; Eisenhower delivered his speech at a time when all eligible American men were legally available to be conscripted. Today, only a small percentage of Americans choose to enroll in the military. The United States does not have compulsory military service and has not used conscription since the early 1970s. (Registration for selective service for men between 18 and 25 was restored in 1980, but no United States citizen has been drafted for nearly forty years.)

The True Costs of Military Spending

At a minimum, then, the degree to which the military steers the American economy and workforce via federal spending seems to have declined since 1961. This does not mean that the MIC has disappeared; neither does it address the broader question of whether our gigantic military budget is wisely allocated or even necessary. The Proxmire critique of the MIC is alive and well; numerous watchdog organizations and some members of Congress (notably Arizona senator John McCain) have continued to document instances of waste and mismanagement in military spending. The decades-long criticisms demonstrate beyond doubt that, as Seymour Melman long argued, excessive cost is built into the Pentagon contracting process. In one classic case, a 1979 review of major weapons systems by the General Accounting Office could not locate a single instance since 1969 in which the Defense Department had not underestimated its costs. In the 1990s, MIC critics began focusing on "add-ons"—money that Congress approves for weapons systems and construction projects even though the Pentagon has not requested it. Perhaps the most notorious example is the C-130 transport plane, manufactured by Lockheed Martin. For decades, Congress approved the purchase of new versions of this plane even though no one from the executive branch had requested them. Over a twenty-year period, only 5 such planes were commissioned by the Air Force; Congress paid for 256.[10]

With billions in military spending taking place with no Pentagon request—and thus presumably without genuine military need—analysts have continually sought other motivations for the perpetuation of wasteful military spending. Typical explanations are that members of Congress act in the perceived interests of their constituencies—the C-130, for instance, is manufactured in Georgia, home to powerful late-twentieth-century legislators like Newt Gingrich and Sam Nunn—and that military spending is valuable even when wasteful, because it creates jobs and enriches the districts where military contracts are fulfilled. Yet these apparent truisms have substantial limits. In a definitive study of military procurement between 1963 and 1995, Barry Rundquist and Thomas Carsey concluded that a military contract does indeed have a discernible effect on a state's income. But they did not find that such spending creates sufficient jobs to affect a state's overall employment rate. Wealthy states with greater capacity to fulfill military contracts are more likely to receive them, and poorer states with high unemployment rates and lower capacity are less likely. Military spending, they found, makes wealthy states wealthier—confirming a thesis put forth in 1970 by Bruce Russett—and heightens inequality among states. That, in turn, leads to greater redistributive spending, which ends up impeding national economic growth.[11]

Such findings were a strand of the critical analysis of the MIC that gained currency during the 1990s: an examination of the economic imbalances created or exacerbated by military spending. Ann Markusen and her colleagues have memorably documented a "gunbelt" of states that receive the lion's share of military contracts. Whereas much military production through the Korean War took place in industrial heartland states—Illinois, Michigan, Ohio, and Pennsylvania—by the 1980s California was by far the largest recipient of Defense Department contracts, with Texas, Florida, and Virginia also playing major roles.[12] (Curiously, Eisenhower's original 1930 industrial mobilization plan recognized the downsides of the geographic concentration of military contracts.) This geographical trend was accelerated by software-heavy military developments such as the Strategic Defense Initiative, and it is now locked in place, Markusen and colleagues maintain, no matter who runs Congress or its committees.

One can experience a frustrating sense that no amount of academic research showing the inefficiency of military spending can change the broader political practice or even the debate. Tens of thousands of pages have been published on the challenges and opportunities of converting the American economy to a civilian footing. In a comprehensive survey of two dozen studies on defense spending and economic growth, Todd Sandler and Keith Hartley concluded that the "net impact of defense on growth is negative, but small."[13] Yet despite decades of research, little consensus exists about the efficiency of the MIC in creating jobs. Claims and counterclaims continue to circulate just as they did in the 1970s, albeit with added urgency after the economic decline of 2009. The Pentagon and its congressional supporters assert that military spending creates vital employment opportunities; opponents respond with detailed studies showing that the same federal dollars invested in clean energy, health care, or education would yield more and better-paying jobs.[14] To a large degree this is economic common sense: a person's labor is bound to be more useful to society if the end product is designed to do something other than explode. And it has been recognized for decades—at least since Eisenhower's "Chance for Peace" speech in 1953—that military spending always carries opportunity costs that keep civilian society from developing in other ways.

This general argument is what defenders of military spending must face. No one disputes that military spending—regardless of its necessity—yields secondary and tertiary benefits in the form of economic stimulus, skilled jobs, industrial spinoffs, worker/researcher training, and the like. It is next to impossible to prove, however, that military spending is the best or most efficient way to create these social goods. This problem also applies to the spinoffs from military spending. In a 2006 review of technologies that have been developed and supported by military budgets, Vernon Ruttan argued that military spending could not be defended as an efficient way to nurture technologies, concluding that "much of military and defense-related technology has been inordinately expensive."[15] Many weary policy analysts have concluded that military spending is simply the socially acceptable form of industrial policy in the United States,[16] with all of industrial policy's bad traits (inefficiency, duplication of effort, political favoritism, the tendency of government to pick losing industries) and none of its good ones (accountability and clearly articulated economic targets).

One reason the debate has moved so little in the past twenty-five years is the lack of a clear alternative to the MIC. The problem isn't theory—there's plenty of theory. But the most visionary work on converting to a civilian economy has usually come from expectations—always dashed—that changing geopolitics would bring about large cuts in military spending. It may be time for critics of the MIC to abandon that fantasy. Barring some extremely unlikely events—a dramatic reduction in perceived threats to the United States, a wholesale rejection of the role of global superpower, or a protracted economic crisis that makes military spending impossible—it is difficult to see how the United States would be sufficiently motivated to eliminate its MIC, let alone replace it with something superior. The United States for the foreseeable future will continue to spend hundreds of billions of dollars every year for military purposes.

Scandals that spotlight ugly issues of military procurement—such as the $1,868 toilet seat and similar outlandish spending that surfaced during the 1980s—often create temporary impetus for limited reform. Such scandals tend to flare up either when the country is relatively at peace or after a military engagement becomes protracted. Many legislative remedies have been passed in the wake of scandals, such as increased requirements for competitive bidding and limits on the revolving door between departing Defense Department personnel and contractors. But scandals have been a recurring feature of the political and military landscape at least since the 1930s, and their reform power recedes as soon as another large conflict looms.

Hence, in the view of many critics, the size and sins of the MIC have grown, not shrunk. As has been shown repeatedly in recent decades, it is exceedingly difficult for the government to take even such seemingly simple actions as closing a few military bases. It is one of the pernicious features of a military-industrial complex that it is nearly impervious to democratic reform. Any systemic change would have to take place in one of two ways. Either the actors in the MIC must decide among themselves to change their methods, or reform must be imposed from outside, assuming there are any powerful forces in American society that are "outside" the MIC.

The former scenario seems highly unlikely. The people responsible for military spending have insufficient incentive to change their procurement methods (which, after all, are not hugely different from the methods of other democracies with large arsenals). This is not to say that the military establishment cannot see the potential benefits of reform. The inefficiency of the MIC is a source of great frustration to Pentagon officials and policymakers. Ballooning costs of weapon systems, for example, mean that even when budgets rise, fewer and fewer weapons can be purchased. Delays in delivery complicate military planning, and of course shoddy materiel costs the lives of soldiers in and out of combat just as it did during the Civil War. Many military contractors would welcome a more streamlined procurement practice, and they could obviously be more profitable if they could spend less on lobbying than they currently do.

Moreover, the broad lack of change in the size and power of the MIC should not obscure the genuine reductions in some aspects of the military's reach. The total number of nuclear weapons in the U.S. arsenal is lower today than at its Cold War peak, as a result of negotiated treaties with Soviet leaders and their post-Communist successors. America has scaled back some of the more redundant reaches of its global military machine, removing nuclear weapons from the Korean peninsula, for example, and reducing its massive postwar troop presence in Germany. During the first year of the Obama administration, Secretary of Defense Robert Gates issued some tough-sounding talk about reprioritizing weapons spending, and many veteran budget watchers were surprised when the administration was able to stop the funding of the F-22 fighter plane.

"World Peace and Human Betterment"

Nonetheless, today's MIC creates problems that cannot simply be resolved with more rational budgets. As we have seen, the perceived definitions of the MIC range much wider than questions of how many guns we buy and for how much. As Eisenhower said in his farewell: "America's leadership and prestige depend, not merely upon our unmatched material progress, riches, and military strength, but on how we use our power in the interests of world peace and human betterment."

The Iraq war has highlighted issues of military accountability, and, as in previous wars, the perception that the military acts with impunity has fed a sense of an MIC exercising unwarranted influence. The conduct of U.S. troops and contractors in Iraq—from administration-approved torture to instances of rape and murder of civilians—are deeply disturbing, and while in many cases individuals have been convicted, the frequency of abuse suggests systemic flaws in the conduct of the war and in the military culture. Such abuses are common during wartime—and the American military behaves far better than most—but the concerns have been heightened by the unprecedented number of private contractors, whose growing influence in military and foreign policy circles has caused some to label them "the fourth branch of government."[17]

The civil liberties component of the garrison state is another troubling area. In an influential and self-described "triumphalist" book called *In the Shadow of the Garrison State*, published in 2000, political scientist Aaron Friedberg—who later joined the Bush administration—argued that America's level of military spending during the Cold War was not only justified, but morally correct. Friedberg postulates that historic mistrust of state power and intentionally "weak" state structures during the Cold War period allowed sufficient accumulation of military

strength "without [the nation] at the same time trans-
forming itself into a garrison state."[18] This thesis has become increasingly difficult to defend in the ensuing decade; indeed, a kind of pattern has emerged in which
martial power has been used to violate civil liberties. During wartime (declared or undeclared), the executive is
often given considerable leeway to detain individuals,
from the curfews and roundups of Asian Americans during World War II to the creation of a large detention
camp at Guantanamo Bay following the attacks of 9/11.
After a certain period, the detentions are challenged and
critical aspects of them are deemed unconstitutional, as
portions of the 2006 Military Commissions Act were
found to be. The multiyear detention of innocent civilians in Guantanamo—labeled "enemy combatants" on
flimsy or false evidence, and denied for too long every
semblance of due process—and instances of government-
sanctioned torture fly in the face of Eisenhower's insistence that American power be used for "world peace and
human betterment."[19] Equally distressing was the extensive surveillance, authorized by the George W. Bush
White House, of U.S. citizens, including warrantless
wiretaps that a federal court held in March 2010 were illegal. Eisenhower would not have anticipated that a perceived threat from Muslim extremists, rather than a per-

ceived threat from Communism, would undermine the reputation of America as a protector of liberty, but he would certainly have recognized the consequences of the military and the executive branch acting in concert to mimic the tactics of a garrison state.

One of the more troubling accusations surrounding the military-industrial complex is that weapons manufacturers influence, or even set, American foreign policy priorities for their own gain. Such accusations, if true, would certainly count as "unwarranted influence." Particularly in recent decades, critics have expanded the MIC's scope beyond the U.S. military to incorporate the arms that American companies sell abroad. The topic of foreign arms sales is arguably closer to the 1930s "merchants of death" thesis than to Eisenhower's speech, since private-sector arms exports were not especially large during his presidency. Nonetheless, the issue is a reasonable extension of the term "military-industrial complex" for two reasons. First, the largest companies selling overseas are the same that contract with the Pentagon—Boeing, General Dynamics, Grumman Northrop, Lockheed Martin, and Raytheon, among others. Second, generally speaking, the export of any significant amount of weapons requires the approval of the United States government, and to get this approval, manufacturers need to exercise influence through channels similar to those they use in their sales to the Pentagon.

Moreover, the explosive growth in the sale of American weapons abroad came about through calculated shifts in government policy. In 1968, Congress passed the Foreign Military Sales Act, which moved the transfer of arms abroad from the realm of foreign aid to the realm of commerce. In 1971, the Nixon administration for the first time created a Pentagon department, called the Defense Security Assistance Agency, designed to approve and help promote arms sales abroad. As a result, arms sales abroad grew rapidly, from under $2 billion a year before the formation of the agency to $5 billion in 1973 and $15 billion in 1975. This happy windfall for military contractors just happened to coincide with the slowdown in Pentagon procurement as the U.S. involvement in Vietnam began to wind down.[20]

In the decades that followed, the United States has become by far the largest arms merchant in the world. Policy analyst William Hartung has documented this monumental rise as well as the troubling ways in which America's foreign policy overlaps with, and is highly influenced by, the overseas agendas of arms manufacturers. There are immense implications for the erosion of human rights, the propping up of corrupt regimes, and the unnecessary exacerbation of global conflict, all of which are obviously damaging to America's image and interests abroad. This problem transcends any question of who is running the White House. America's domination of the worldwide weapons bazaar has continued despite the global economic slowdown of 2008 and 2009. In 2009, the United States not only heftily increased its arms sales abroad—to $37.8 billion—but also increased its share to more than two-thirds of all armament deals, according to the Congressional Research Service.[21]

Taken collectively, these contemporary problems constitute an overreaching military-industrial complex at least equal to the one Eisenhower warned against. Trimming around the edges of the massive military budget is unlikely to have much effect on these problems. What is required is political pressure from what Eisenhower labeled "an alert and knowledgeable citizenry," perhaps some version of the popular outrage that since 2008 has been focused on issues such as Wall Street bonuses. Still more crucial is courageous leadership from political and social leaders able to identify dangerous rifts in our system, as Eisenhower did a half century ago.

Eisenhower's Farewell Address

Delivered January 17, 1961. This is a transcript from an audio file of the speech.

Good evening, my fellow Americans.

First, I should like to express my gratitude to the radio and television networks for the opportunities they have given me over the years to bring reports and messages to our nation. My special thanks go to them for the opportunity of addressing you this evening. Three days from now, after half a century in the service of our country, I shall lay down the responsibilities of office as, in traditional and solemn ceremony, the authority of the presidency is vested in my successor. This evening, I come to you with a message of leave-taking and farewell, and to share a few final thoughts with you, my countrymen. Like every other—Like every other citizen, I wish the new president, and all who will labor with him, Godspeed. I pray that the coming years will be blessed with peace and prosperity for all.

Our people expect their president and the Congress to find essential agreement on issues of great moment, the wise resolution of which will better shape the future of the nation. My own relations with the Congress, which began on a remote and tenuous basis when, long ago, a member of the Senate appointed me to West Point, have since ranged to the intimate during the war and immediate postwar period, and finally to the mutually interdependent during these past eight years. In this final relationship, the Congress and the administration have, on most vital issues, cooperated well, to serve the nation good, rather than mere partisanship, and so have assured that the business of the nation should go forward. So, my official relationship with the Congress ends in a feeling—on my part—of gratitude that we have been able to do so much together.

We now stand ten years past the midpoint of a century that has witnessed four major wars among great nations. Three of these involved our own country. Despite these holocausts, America is today the strongest, the most influential, and most productive nation in the world. Understandably proud of this pre-eminence, we yet realize that America's leadership and prestige depend, not merely upon our unmatched material progress, riches, and military strength, but on how we use our power in the interests of world peace and human betterment.

Throughout America's adventure in free government, our basic purposes have been to keep the peace, to foster progress in human achievement, and to enhance liberty, dignity, and integrity among peoples and among nations. To strive for less would be unworthy of a free and religious people. Any failure traceable to arrogance, or our lack of comprehension, or readiness to sacrifice would inflict upon us grievous hurt, both at home and abroad.

Progress toward these noble goals is persistently threatened by the conflict now engulfing the world. It commands our whole attention, absorbs our very beings. We face a hostile ideology global in scope, atheistic in character, ruthless in purpose, and insiduous [insidious] in method. Unhappily, the danger it poses promises to be of indefinite duration. To meet it successfully, there is called for, not so much the emotional and transitory sacrifices of crisis, but rather those which enable us to carry forward steadily, surely, and without complaint the burdens of a prolonged and complex struggle with liberty the stake.

Only thus shall we remain, despite every provocation, on our charted course toward permanent peace and human betterment.

Crises there will continue to be. In meeting them, whether foreign or domestic, great or small, there is a recurring temptation to feel that some spectacular and costly action could become the miraculous solution to all current difficulties. A huge increase in newer elements of our defenses; development of unrealistic programs to cure every ill in agriculture; a dramatic expansion in basic and applied research—these and many other possibilities, each possibly promising in itself, may be suggested as the only way to the road we wish to travel.

But each proposal must be weighed in the light of a broader consideration: the need to maintain balance in and among national programs, balance between the private and the public economy, balance between the cost and hoped for advantages, balance between the clearly necessary and the comfortably desirable, balance between our essential requirements as a nation and the duties imposed by the nation upon the individual, balance between actions of the moment and the national welfare of the future. Good judgment seeks balance and progress. Lack of it eventually finds imbalance and frustration. The record of many decades stands as proof that our people and their government have, in the main, understood these truths and have responded to them well, in the face of threat and stress.

But threats, new in kind or degree, constantly arise. Of these, I mention two only.

A vital element in keeping the peace is our military establishment. Our arms must be mighty, ready for instant action, so that no potential aggressor may be tempted to risk his own destruction. Our military organization today bears little relation to that known of any of my predecessors in peacetime, or, indeed, by the fighting men of World War II or Korea.

Until the latest of our world conflicts, the United States had no armaments industry. American makers of plowshares could, with time and as required, make swords as well. But we can no longer risk emergency improvisation of national defense. We have been compelled to create a permanent armaments industry of vast proportions. Added to this, three and a half million men and women are directly engaged in the defense establishment. We annually spend on military security alone more than the net income of all United States cooperations—corporations.

Now this conjunction of an immense military establishment and a large arms industry is new in the American experience. The total influence—economic, political, even spiritual—is felt in every city, every statehouse, every office of the federal government. We recognize the imperative need for this development. Yet, we must not fail to comprehend its grave implications. Our toil, resources, and livelihood are all involved. So is the very structure of our society.

In the councils of government, we must guard against the acquisition of unwarranted influence, whether sought or unsought, by the military-industrial complex. The potential for the disastrous rise of misplaced power exists and will persist. We must never let the weight of this combination endanger our liberties or democratic processes. We should take nothing for granted. Only an alert and knowledgeable citizenry can compel the proper meshing of the huge industrial and military machinery of defense with our peaceful methods and goals, so that security and liberty may prosper together. Akin to, and largely responsible for the sweeping changes in our industrial-military posture, has been the technological revolution during recent decades. In this revolution, research has become central; it also becomes more formalized, complex, and costly. A steadily increasing share is conducted for, by, or at the direction of, the federal government.

Today, the solitary inventor, tinkering in his shop, has been overshadowed by task forces of scientists in laboratories and testing fields. In the same fashion, the free university, historically the fountainhead of free ideas and scientific discovery, has experienced a revolution in the conduct of research. Partly because of the huge costs involved, a government contract becomes virtually a substitute for intellectual curiosity. For every old blackboard there are now hundreds of new electronic computers. The prospect of domination of the nation's scholars by federal employment, project allocations, and the power of money is ever present—and is gravely to be regarded. Yet, in holding scientific research and discovery in respect, as we should, we must also be alert to the equal and opposite danger that public policy could itself become the captive of a scientific-technological elite.

It is the task of statesmanship to mold, to balance, and to integrate these and other forces, new and old, within the principles of our democratic system—ever aiming toward the supreme goals of our free society.

Another factor in maintaining balance involves the element of time. As we peer into society's future, we—you and I, and our government—must avoid the impulse to live only for today, plundering for our own ease and convenience the precious resources of tomorrow. We cannot mortgage the material assets of our grandchildren without risking the loss also of their political and spiritual heritage. We want democracy to survive for all generations to come, not to become the insolvent phantom of tomorrow.

During the long lane of the history yet to be written, America knows that this world of ours, ever growing smaller, must avoid becoming a community of dreadful fear and hate, and be, instead, a proud confederation of mutual trust and respect. Such a confederation must be one of equals. The weakest must come to the conference table with the same confidence as do we, protected as we are by our moral, economic, and military strength. That table, though scarred by many fast frustrations— past frustrations, cannot be abandoned for the certain agony of disarmament—of the battlefield.

Disarmament, with mutual honor and confidence, is a continuing imperative. Together we must learn how to compose differences, not with arms, but with intellect and decent purpose. Because this need is so sharp and apparent, I confess that I lay down my official responsibilities in this field with a definite sense of disappointment. As one who has witnessed the horror and the lingering sadness of war, as one who knows that another war could utterly destroy this civilization which has been so slowly and painfully built over thousands of years, I wish I could say tonight that a lasting peace is in sight. Happily, I can say that war has been avoided. Steady progress toward our ultimate goal has been made. But so much remains to be done. As a private citizen, I shall never cease to do what little I can to help the world advance along that road.

So, in this, my last good night to you as your president, I thank you for the many opportunities you have given me for public service in war and in peace. I trust in that—in that—in that service you find some things worthy. As for the rest of it, I know you will find ways to improve performance in the future.

You and I, my fellow citizens, need to be strong in our faith that all nations, under God, will reach the goal of peace with justice. May we be ever unswerving in devotion to principle, confident but humble with power, diligent in pursuit of the nations' great goals. To all the peoples of the world, I once more give expression to America's prayerful and continuing aspiration: We pray that peoples of all faiths, all races, all nations, may have their great human needs satisfied; that those now denied opportunity shall come to enjoy it to the full; that all who yearn for freedom may experience its few spiritual blessings. Those who have freedom will understand, also, its heavy responsibility; that all who are insensitive to the needs of others will learn charity; and that the sources—scourges of poverty, disease, and ignorance will be made [to] disappear from the earth; and that in the goodness of time, all peoples will come to live together in a peace guaranteed by the binding force of mutual respect and love.

Now, on Friday noon, I am to become a private citizen. I am proud to do so. I look forward to it.

Thank you, and good night.

Notes

ABBREVIATIONS

AWF   Ann Whitman File, Eisenhower Library
COH   Columbia Oral History Collection
EL   Eisenhower Library
PPP   Public Papers of the Presidents (published annually by Na-
      tional Archives and Records Service, Washington, D.C.)

ONE
Tracking the Unwarranted Influence

1. Eisenhower made the comment to C. D. Jackson, as recounted
    in Robert Schlesinger, *White House Ghosts: Presidents and Their
    Speechwriters From FDR to George W. Bush* (New York: Simon
    and Schuster, 2008), p. 94.
2. See Ira Chernus, *Eisenhower's Atoms for Peace* (College Station:
    Texas A&M University Press, 2002).
3. Kevin Mattson, *What the Heck Are You Up To, Mr. President:
    Jimmy Carter, America's 'Malaise,' and the Speech That Should
    Have Changed the Country* (New York, Bloomsbury, 2009), and

Romesh Ratnesar, *Tear Down This Wall: A City, a President, and the Speech That Ended the Cold War* (New York: Simon and Schuster, 2009).

4. Alex Roland, "The Military-Industrial Complex: Lobby and Trope," in *The Long War: A New History of U.S. National Security Policy Since World War II* (New York: Columbia University Press, 2007), pp. 335–370.

5. There are exceptions to this generalization, notably Murray Weidenbaum and many libertarian critics, who oppose the excesses of the MIC as part of a broader opposition to large government.

6. Derek Leebaert, *The Fifty-Year Wound: The True Price of America's Cold War Victory* (New York: Little Brown, 2002), p. xiii.

7. As an exception, one notable true defender of the MIC was John Stanley Baumgartner, author of *The Lonely Warriors: The Case for the Military-Industrial Complex* (Los Angeles: Nash, 1970).

TWO

Intellectual Origins

1. I have located three uses of the phrase "military-industrial complex" prior to Eisenhower's 1961 speech. In two of those instances, the term is used to describe a specific physical part of a country, a "compound" as much as a "complex." In the first case, it was a steel-producing region east of the Ural Mountains in the Soviet Union (H. R. Knickerbocker, "The Soviet Five-Year Plan," *International Affairs*, vol. 10, no. 4 [July 1931], p. 442); in the second case, a Confederate arms and shipping stronghold around the port of Shreveport during the U.S. Civil War (Waldo W. Moore, "The Defense of Shreveport: The Confederacy's Last Redoubt," *Military Affairs*, Volume 17, Issue 2 [Summer 1953], 72–82.)

The third usage, however, refers to World War II and is much closer to the sense in which Eisenhower used the term. The author—the economist and diplomat Winfield W. Riefler, writing in *Foreign Affairs*—specifically discusses the role of industrial output in determining the outcome of the war, and lays out the intersection between civilian and military components of an economy necessary for "a military-industrial complex to function." Given the subject matter, the prominence of the author, and the prestige of the journal involved, it seems likely that someone in Eisenhower's advisory circle—possibly Eisenhower himself—would have read this article, but I have found no specific connection between it and Eisenhower's farewell speech. See Winfield W. Riefler, "Our Economic Contribution to Victory," *Foreign Affairs*, vol. 26, no. 1 (October 1947), pp. 90–103.

2. C. Wright Mills, *The Power Elite* (1956; reprint, New York: Oxford University Press, 2000), pp. 7–8.

3. See, for example, chapter 1 of Paul A. C. Koistinen, *The Military-Industrial Complex: A Historical Perspective* (New York: Praeger, 1980). Another useful summary of disarmament thinking and its relationship to the MIC is Earl A. Molander, "Historical Antecedents of Military-Industrial Criticism," in *War, Business and American Society: Historical Perspectives on the Military-Industrial Complex*, ed. Benjamin Franklin Cooling (Port Washington, New York: Kennikat Press, 1977), pp. 171–187.

4. H. C. Engelbrecht and F. C. Hanighen, *Merchants of Death* (New York: Dodd Mead, 1934), p. 2.

5. *Congressional Record*, February 15, 1915, cited in George Seldes, *Iron, Blood and Profits* (New York: Harper and Brothers, 1934), p. 18.

6. Kurt Hackemer, *The U.S. Navy and the Origins of the Military-Industrial Complex, 1847–83* (Annapolis: Naval Institute Press, 2001), chapter 1.

7. This citation is from the *Congressional Record*, February 15, 1915, and reproduced as Appendix V in Seldes, *Iron, Blood and Profits*.

8. "Book Notes," *New York Times*, April 5, 1934.

9. The best summary of Nye's career and the dramatic rise and fall of his munitions inquiry is in Wayne S. Cole, *Senator Gerald P. Nye and American Foreign Relations* (Minneapolis: University of Minnesota Press, 1962).

10. Cole, *Senator Gerald P. Nye*, p. 89.
11. The most complete account of the UDC's history and influence is Marvin Swartz, *The Union of Democratic Control in British Politics During the First World War* (Oxford: Clarendon Press, 1971).
12. One military history that influenced the UDC's economic critique was I. S. Bloch, *Modern Weapons and Modern War*, trans. W. T. Stead (London: Grant Richards, 1900).
13. Henry Noel Brailsford, *The War of Steel and Gold* (London: G. Bell and Sons, 1914), p. 309.
14. A detailed account of the ties between Wilson's advisors and the UDC can be found in Henry Pelling, *America and the British Left, from Bright to Bevan* (London: Adam and Charles Black, 1956).
15. Arthur Walworth, *Woodrow Wilson* (2nd ed., revised; Boston: Houghton Mifflin, 1965), book II, p. 2.
16. "WPB Aide Urges U.S. To Keep War Set-Up," *The New York Times*, January 20, 1944.
17. Walter H. Waggoner, "Strategic Hoard," *Wall Street Journal*, January 6, 1944.
18. From the introduction to Walter J. Oakes, "Toward a Permanent War Economy?" *Politics*, February 1944.
19. Forrest Reserve Black, "The Profits of War," *The Nation*, vol. 131, no. 3399 (August 27, 1930), p. 222.
20. Eisenhower's involvement in this exchange is documented in Daniel D. Holt and James W. Leyerzapf, eds., *Eisenhower: The Prewar Diaries and Selected Papers, 1905–1941* (Baltimore: Johns Hopkins University Press, 1998), pp. 143–144.
21. Hanson W. Baldwin, "Secretary of Defense Takes Office in Era of International Uncertainty," *New York Times*, September 21, 1947.
22. An abridged version of "The Garrison State" is republished in Harold D. Lasswell, *Harold D. Lasswell on Political Sociology*, ed. Dwaine Marvick (Chicago: University of Chicago Press, 1977), pp. 165–176.
23. "U.S. Seen Becoming a 'Garrison State,'" *New York Times*, October 12, 1950.
24. "The President's News Conference of May 14, 1953," PPP, 1953, doc. 77, pp. 293–294.

25. "Radio Address to the American People on the National Security and Its Costs," May 19, 1953, PPP, 1953, doc. 82, p. 310.

26. Alex Roland has specifically discussed Eisenhower's fear of a garrison state as a precursor to the concept of a military-industrial complex. See "The Grim Paraphernalia: Eisenhower and the Garrison State," in Dennis E. Showalter, ed., *Forging the Shield: Eisenhower and National Security for the 21st Century* (Chicago: Imprint Publications, 2005), pp. 13–22.

27. Malcolm Moos, *The Republicans: A History of Their Party* (New York: Random House, 1956), p. 495.

28. Mills, *Power Elite*, p. 361.

THREE

War, Peace, and Eisenhower

1. Stephen E. Ambrose, *Eisenhower: Soldier, General of the Army, President-Elect, 1890–1952* (New York: Simon and Schuster, 1983), p. 16.

2. An important exception is Kerry E. Irish, "Apt Pupil: Dwight Eisenhower and the 1930 Industrial Mobilization Plan," *The Journal of Military History* 70 (January 2006), pp. 31–61.

3. Ambrose, *Eisenhower*, p. 92.

4. A fine summary of the politics and work of the War Policies Commission can be found in Stuart Dean Brandes, *Warhogs: A History of War Profits in America* (Lexington: University Press of Kentucky, 1997), pp. 205 ff.

5. Charles J. V. Murphy, "The Eisenhower Shift," *Fortune*, January 1956, p. 85.

6. John Lewis Gaddis, *Strategies of Containment* (revised and expanded ed.; New York: Oxford University Press, 2005), p. 130.

7. Frederick H. Payne, "Fundamentals of Industrial Mobilization," *Army Ordnance* 11 (July–August 1930), pp. 7–8.

8. "Brief History of Planning for Procurement and Industrial Mobilization," October 2, 1931, reprinted in Daniel D. Holt and James W. Leyerzapf, eds., *Eisenhower: The Prewar Diaries and Selected Papers, 1905–1941* (Baltimore: Johns Hopkins University Press), p. 184.

9. "Fundamentals of Industrial Mobilization," memorandum from

Eisenhower to Frederick H. Payne, June 16, 1930, reprinted in Daniel D. Holt and James W. Leyerzapf, eds., *Eisenhower: The Prewar Diaries and Selected Papers, 1905–1941*, p. 141.

10. The 1930 Industrial Mobilization Plan, National Archives and Records Administration, RG-107, Box 12, File 110, p. 54.

11. Dwight D. Eisenhower, *Crusade in Europe* (Garden City, New York: Doubleday, 1948), p. 443.

12. Letter from Dwight Eisenhower to Everett E. Hazlett, November 27, 1945, reprinted in Robert W. Griffith, ed., *Ike's Letters to a Friend 1941–1958* (Lawrence: University Press of Kansas, 1984), pp. 27–31.

13. Letter from Dwight Eisenhower to Everett E. Hazlett, April 27, 1949, in Griffith, *Ike's Letters*, pp. 53–55.

14. "Eisenhower Backs Property Rights," *New York Times*, September 22, 1948.

15. Chester J. Pach, Jr., and Elmo Richardson, *The Presidency of Dwight D. Eisenhower* (Lawrence, Kansas: University Press of Kansas, 1991), p. 53.

16. Figures cited in Murphy, "Eisenhower Shift," p. 87.

17. The discussion of the divisions within the Eisenhower administration owes much to H. W. Brands's article "The Age of Vulnerability: Eisenhower and the National Insecurity State," *American Historical Review*, vol. 94, no. 4 (October 1989), pp. 963–989.

18. Charles J. V. Murphy, "Eisenhower's White House," *Fortune*, July 1953, p. 176.

19. Gaddis, *Strategies of Containment*, p. 132.

20. Useful discussions of the rationales behind, and implications of, NSC 162/2 can be found in Brands, "Age of Vulnerability"; Pach and Richardson, *Presidency of Dwight D. Eisenhower*, chapter 4; Gaddis, *Strategies of Containment*, chapters 5–6; Ira Chernus, *Eisenhower's Atoms for Peace* (College Station: Texas A&M University Press, 2002), pp. 56 ff.; and Warner R. Schilling, Paul Y. Hammond, and Glenn H. Snyder, *Strategy, Politics and Defense Budgets* (New York: Columbia University Press, 1962).

21. John Foster Dulles, "The Evolution of Foreign Policy," Before the Council of Foreign Relations, New York, *Department of State, Press Release No. 81*, January 12, 1954.

22. NSC 162/2, "A Report to the National Security Council," October 30, 1953, p. 1. A copy of NSC 162/2 can be found at the Federation of American Scientists website, http://www.fas.org/irp/offdocs/nsc-hst/nsc-162-2.pdf.

23. Department of the Air Force Appropriations for 1954, Hearings before the Committee on Appropriations, House of Representatives, 83d Cong., 1st Sess. (Washington, 1953), p. 961.

24. Brands, "Age of Vulnerability," p. 989.

25. The earliest declassified document pertaining to Project Candor is dated July 22, 1953, and can be found at the Eisenhower Library: White House Office, National Security Council Papers, PSB Central Files Series, Box 17, PSB 091.4 U.S. (2).

26. "President Says Atom Bomb Would Be Used Like 'Bullet,'" *New York Times*, March 17, 1955.

27. Dwight D. Eisenhower, *Mandate for Change* (Garden City, New York: Doubleday, 1963), p. 181.

28. Ira Chernus has repeatedly used the term "apocalypse management," both as the title of a 2008 book (*Apocalypse Management: Eisenhower and the Discourse of National Insecurity*, Stanford University Press), and as a frame for his 2002 book *Eisenhower's Atoms for Peace*. While many have used the phrase "national insecurity state," it was most influentially deployed by H. W. Brands's 1989 "Age of Vulnerability" essay.

29. Memorandum, Paul Nitze to Secretary Dulles, "General Considerations Relating to the Draft Presidential Speech," April 2, 1953; John Foster Dulles Papers, EL, Draft Presidential Correspondence and Speech Series, Box 1, President's Speech April, 1953.

30. PPP, 1953, doc. 50, pp. 179 ff.

31. Blanche Wiesen Cook, *The Declassified Eisenhower* (New York: Penguin Books, 1984), pp. 180–181.

32. John Emmet Hughes, *The Ordeal of Power: A Political Memoir of the Eisenhower Years* (New York: Atheneum, 1963), p. 122.

33. Memorandum, President Eisenhower to C. D. Jackson, December 31, 1953, AWF, DDE Diary Series, Box 4, DDE Diary December 1953 (1).

34. The account of the world government and early antinuclear movement relies on Milton S. Katz, *Ban the Bomb: A History of*

SANE, the Committee for a Sane Nuclear Policy, 1957–1985 (New York: Greenwood Press, 1986).

35. "8000 At Rally Here For World Unity," *New York Times*, June 10, 1949.

36. Norman Cousins, *Modern Man Is Obsolete* (New York: Viking, 1945). The best biography of Cousins is Milton Katz's chapter in Charles DeBenedetti, ed., *Peace Heroes in Twentieth-Century America* (Bloomington: University of Indiana Press, 1986), pp. 169–197.

37. Norman Cousins, *The Pathology of Power* (New York: W. W. Norton, 1987), p. 71.

38. Letter from Eisenhower to Norman Cousins, May 30, 1959, in *The Papers of Dwight David Eisenhower* (Baltimore: Johns Hopkins University Press, 1996), volume 20, doc. 1182, p. 1504.

39. See, for example, David Serlin, *Replaceable You: Engineering the Body in Postwar America* (Chicago: University of Chicago Press, 2004), pp. 66–67, and Rodney Barker, *The Hiroshima Maidens* (New York: Penguin Books, 1986), pp. 81–82.

FOUR

Eisenhower's Contentious Second Term

1. "Think of a Man," *Saturday Review*, August 4, 1956, pp. 9–14.

2. Letter from Eisenhower to Norman Cousins, August 6, 1956, *The Papers of Dwight David Eisenhower* (Baltimore: Johns Hopkins University Press, 1996), volume 17, doc. 1939.

3. Arthur Larson, *Eisenhower: The President Nobody Knew* (New York: Scribner's, 1968), pp. 172–173.

4. The Reminiscences of Malcolm Moos 1972, p. 23, COH.

5. AWF, DDE Diary Series, Box 29, Telephone calls, November 18, 1957.

6. "Excerpts from Message By Schweitzer," *New York Times*, April 24, 1957.

7. A thorough account of the Schweitzer statement and the subsequent debate can be found in Robert A. Divine, *Blowing on the Wind: The Nuclear Test Ban Debate 1954–1960* (New York: Oxford University Press, 1978), pp. 121 ff.

8. "Meeting the Threat of Surprise Attack: Technological Capabilities of the Science Advisory Committee," February 14,

1955, cited in Blanche Wiesen Cook, *The Declassified Eisenhower* (New York: Penguin Books, 1984), p. 168.

9. "Outlawing the Atom, Defending the West," *Newsweek*, May 6, 1957, pp. 51–57.

10. Letter marked "Personal and Confidential" from Dwight D. Eisenhower to Norman Cousins, July 9, 1957, Norman Cousins papers in UCLA Special Collections, Coll. 1385, Box 269, Folder 1957—Dwight Eisenhower.

11. Charles J. V. Murphy, "The White House Since Sputnik," *Fortune*, January 1958, p. 98.

12. Murphy, "White House Since Sputnik," p. 100.

13. EL, Arthur Larson papers, Box 3, President's Speeches: Science & Security: Background material folder.

14. AWF, DDE Diary Series, Box 29, Telephone calls, November 21, 1957.

15. Harold Stassen and Marshall Houts, *Eisenhower: Turning the World Toward Peace* (St. Paul, Minnesota: Merrill/Magnus Publishing Corporation, 1990), pp. 236–237.

16. Robert Hotz, "Sputnik in the Sky," *Aviation Week*, October 14, 1957, p. 21.

17. Reminiscences of Malcolm Moos, p. 34.

18. James R. Killian, *Sputnik, Scientists and Eisenhower* (Cambridge, Massachusetts: MIT Press, 1977), p. 238.

19. "Transcript of Eisenhower's News Conference on Domestic and Foreign Affairs," *New York Times*, January 19, 1961.

20. Notes on Legislative Leadership Meeting, June 2, 1959; in AWF, DDE Diary Series, Box 42, Staff Notes June 1–15, 1959 (2).

21. Jack Raymond, "President Says 'Munitions Lobby' Stirs His Concern," *New York Times*, June 4, 1959; Killian, *Sputnik, Scientists and Eisenhower*, p. 230.

22. Memorandum of Conference with the President, A. J. Goodpaster, June 9, 1959; in AWF, DDE Diary Series, Box 42.

23. Memorandum of Conference with the President, A. J. Goodpaster, July 14, 1959; in AWF, DDE Diary Series, Box 43.

24. AWF, DDE Diary Series, Box 34, Telephone calls—July 1958.

25. "Air Chief Scores B-70 Cut; Plans Appeal to Congress," *New York Times*, January 12, 1960.

26. AWF, DDE Diary Series, Box 47, Telephone Calls, January 1960.

27. Address at the Republican National Convention in Chicago, July 26, 1960, *Public Papers of the Presidents*, Dwight D. Eisenhower, 1960, doc. 245.

28. A summary of the development of Eisenhower's enthusiasm for student exchange, and the tepid reactions of many of his advisors, can be found in Walter L. Hixson, *Parting the Curtain: Propaganda, Culture, and the Cold War, 1945–1961* (Houndmills: Macmillan, 1997), pp. 101 ff.

29. Telephone conversation, Dwight Eisenhower and Milton Eisenhower, March 14, 1958, AWF, DDE Diary Series, Box 31, Telephone calls, March 1958. Milton also mentions this idea, calling it "half serious," in his memoir *The President Is Calling* (New York: Doubleday, 1974), p. 359.

30. EL, Arthur Larson papers, Box 5, March 13, 1958, American Society of Newspaper Editors, April 17, 1958, Draft #3.

FIVE

The Speech

1. Blanche Wiesen Cook, *The Declassified Eisenhower* (New York: Penguin Books, 1984), p. xviii.

2. Stephen E. Ambrose, *Eisenhower: The President* (New York: Simon and Schuster, 1984), pp. 611–612.

3. Geoffrey Perret, *Eisenhower* (New York: Random House, 1999), p. 599. Perret's assertion appears to be sourced—in chapter 44, footnote 37—to "Andrew J. Goodpaster interview, EL," that is, the oral history interview that originates with the Eisenhower Library. A full transcript of that interview can be found at http://www.eisenhower.archives.gov/Research/Oral_Histories/oral_history_transcripts/Goodpaster_Andrew_378.pdf; however, while Goodpaster acknowledges Eisenhower's frustration with Congress, he makes no claim about any phrasing in any draft of the farewell speech, nor any phrasing being removed.

4. Douglas Brinkley, "Eisenhower," *American Heritage Magazine*, vol. 52, issue 6 (September 2001). In an e-mail exchange with the author, Brinkley wrote: "Back when I was director of the Eisenhower Center I interviewed Mr. Killian about the speech,"

and Killian "was very specific with me" about objecting to the phrase "military-industrial-scientific" in a draft of the speech. This is a curiously unsubstantiated claim on several levels. For one, Brinkley's dates are evidently confused: Killian died in January 1988, and Brinkley did not become director of the Eisenhower Center until 2002, more than fourteen years later. Furthermore, Killian's own memoir not only does not mention any objection to the phrase, it does not indicate that Killian ever saw the speech prior to its delivery; neither does Killian's Presidential Library oral history. No other known participant in the drafting of the speech has indicated that this phrase existed, much less that it was criticized. And no extant draft indicates it, either. In a subsequent e-mail, Brinkley said that he had heard this story from journalist Carl Rowan, who supposedly heard it from Killian. Brinkley says he did not ask Rowan to verify the claim, and I can find no corroborating source for it.

5. The most complete assembly of the relevant documents around the speech is in Charles J. G. Griffin, "New Light on Eisenhower's Farewell Address," *Presidential Studies Quarterly*, vol. 22, issue 3 (Summer 1992), pp. 469–479.

6. The Reminisces of Malcolm Moos 1972, COH, p. 33.

7. Letter, DDE to Milton Stover Eisenhower, May 25, 1959, The Papers of Dwight D. Eisenhower, volume 20, doc. 1172, pp. 1492–1493.

8. Memorandum for file, October 31, 1960; in EL, Ralph Williams papers, Box 1, Chronological (1) Folder.

9. This anecdote is in Moos's Columbia oral history, as well as in "Ike's Historic 1961 Warning," *Chicago Daily News*, April 14, 1969.

10. Thomas I. Cook and Malcolm Moos, *Power Through Purpose: The Realism of Idealism as a Basis for Foreign Policy* (Baltimore: The Johns Hopkins University Press, 1954), pp. 159–160.

11. Reminisces of Malcolm Moos, COH, p. 33.

12. "Ex-Officers Face Defense-Job Curb," *New York Times*, January 18, 1960.

13. Oral History of Ralph Williams (OH-503), EL, 1988, p. 35.

14. Malcolm Moos, *Dwight D. Eisenhower* (New York: Random House, 1964), p. 166.

15. Milton Eisenhower, *The President Is Calling* (New York: Doubleday, 1974), p. 322.
16. Letter from Ralph E. Williams to Martin Teasley, December 28, 1985; EL, Ralph Williams papers, Box 1.
17. Letter from Ralph E. Williams to Martin Teasley, October 28, 1986; EL, Ralph Williams papers, Box 1.
18. Ira Chernus, *Eisenhower's Atoms For Peace* (College Station: Texas A&M University Press, 2002), p. 124.
19. DDE Diary Series, January 24, 1958; Box 29, January 1958.
20. Geoffrey Perret, *A Country Made by War* (New York: 1989), p. 480.
21. Piers Brendon, *Ike: The Life and Times of Dwight D. Eisenhower* (London: Secker and Warburg, 1987), p. 9.
22. Martin J. Medhurst, "Reconceptualizing Rhetorical History: Eisenhower's Farewell Address," *Quarterly Journal of Speech* 80 (1994), pp. 207–208.
23. The text of the 1960 Republican platform can be found at John T. Woolley and Gerhard Peters, *The American Presidency Project*, University of California, Santa Barbara, http://www.presidency.ucsb.edu/ws/index.php?pid=25839.
24. Letter from Williams to Teasley, December 28, 1985.
25. Martin J. Medhurst, "Robert L. Scott Plays Dwight D. Eisenhower," *Quarterly Journal of Speech* 81 (1995), pp. 502–503.
26. Malcolm Moos, "The Need to Know and the Right to Tell," *Political Science Quarterly*, vol. 79, no. 2 (June 1964), p. 182; Walter Lippmann, "Eisenhower's Farewell Warning," *Washington Post*, January 19, 1961.
27. Jack Raymond, "The Military-Industrial Complex: An Analysis," *New York Times*, January 22, 1961.
28. Unsigned editorial, *The Nation*, January 28, 1961, pp. 69–70.

SIX

Interpretations and Embellishments

1. Martin J. Medhurst, "Robert L. Scott Plays Dwight D. Eisenhower," *Quarterly Journal of Speech* 81 (1995), pp. 502–503. This brief Medhurst essay was a response to Robert L. Scott's "Eisen-

hower's Farewell Address: Response to Medhurst," *QJS* 81 (1995), pp. 496–501, which itself was a reply to Medhurst's more significant article "Reconceptualizing Rhetorical History: Eisenhower's Farewell Address," *QJS* 80 (1994), pp. 195–218.

2. Alex Roland, "The Military-Industrial Complex: Lobby and Trope," in A. J. Bacevich, ed., *The Long War: A New History of U.S. National Security Since World War II* (New York: Columbia University Press, 2007), p. 345.

3. Robert S. McNamara, *Blundering Into Disaster: Surviving the First Century of the Nuclear Age* (New York: Pantheon Books, 1986), p. 44.

4. "Text of President Kennedy's Special Message to Congress on Defense Spending," *New York Times*, March 29, 1961.

5. McNamara, *Blundering Into Disaster*, p. 55. The memorandum in question has been declassified and can be read on the Defense Department website: http://www.dod.mil/pubs/foi/reading_room/ 334.pdf. The LeMay anecdote is related in Fred Kaplan, *The Wizards of Armageddon* (New York: Simon and Schuster, 1983), pp. 132–133.

6. A detailed compilation of McNamara's battles with military personnel and members of Congress can be found in Chapter 5 of Julius Duscha, *Arms, Money and Politics* (New York: Ives Washburn, 1965), pp. 86–113.

7. A succinct account of the clash over the B-70 is in chapter 7 of Nick Kotz, *Wild Blue Yonder: Money, Politics and the B-1 Bomber* (New York: Pantheon, 1988).

8. *Economic Impacts of Disarmament*, United States Arms Control and Disarmament Agency publication 2 (Washington, D.C.: U.S. Government Printing Office), pp. 3–4.

9. Marquis Childs, "Invisible Lobby Behind the RS-70," *Washington Post*, March 26, 1962; James Reston, "Washington: On Getting Run Over by a Gravy Train," *New York Times*, March 15, 1963.

10. Dwight D. Eisenhower, *Waging Peace: 1956–1961* (Garden City, New York: Doubleday, 1965), pp. 252, 615.

11. Earl Warren, "The Bill of Rights and the Military," *New York University Law Review* 37 (1962), p. 182.

12. The background to these cases can be found in Ronald Takaki,

Strangers from a Different Shore (New York: Little, Brown, 1998), pp. 385 ff.

13. *Hirabayashi v. United States*, 320 U.S. 81 (1943), p. 320 U.S. 101. The text of the decision is reproduced at Justia.com: http://supreme.justia.com/us/320/81/case.html.

14. The complete text of the Port Huron Statement is reproduced at http://coursesa.matrix.msu.edu/~hst306/documents/huron.html, as well as in an appendix to James Miller, *Democracy Is in the Streets* (Cambridge, Massachusetts: Harvard University Press, 1994).

15. The question of when the New Left began and what precisely constituted it is complicated, varies between countries, and is beyond the scope of this book. The journal *New Left Review* began publishing in Great Britain in 1960; its focus was Marxist theory, Labour politics, and the development of socialism outside of Stalinist influence. In the United States, the focus of the New Left was generally less explicitly Marxist, and it could be said to have begun with the formation of Students for a Democratic Society in 1960. However, the American New Left also blended in (as well as clashed) with the civil rights movement, the women's liberation movement, and other protest movements, and so determining its date of origin depends to a considerable degree on how it is defined.

16. Tom Hayden, *Rebel* (Los Angeles: Red Hen Press, 2003), p. 71. While of course other leaders of the New Left had their own, and different influences—Hayden also cites Camus—Hayden's memoir is a persuasive account of the dominant influence of Mills.

17. "This conjunction of an immense military establishment and a large arms industry is new in the American experience. The total influence—economic, political, even spiritual—is felt in every city, every statehouse, every office of the federal government. We recognize the imperative need for this development. Yet we must not fail to comprehend its grave implications. Our toil, resources and livelihood are all involved; so is the very structure of our society."

18. Martin Luther King, Jr., "Transformed Nonconformist," in

Strength to Love (Philadelphia: Fortress Press, 1981), p. 24. According to King scholars, early published editions of this sermon deleted King's antimilitaristic stances. The most definitive version of the sermon and the various alterations made to it is in Clayborne Carson, ed., *The Papers of Martin Luther King*, vol. VI: *Advocate of the Social Gospel* (Berkeley: University of California Press, 2007), pp. 466 ff.

19. "Eisenhower's Letter to Senate Group," *Washington Post*, January 24, 1962.

20. A transcript and recording of Savio's speech can be found at AmericanRhetoric.com, http://www.americanrhetoric.com/speeches/mariosaviosproulhallsitin.htm.

21. The Free Speech Movement sprung up on the Berkeley campus in 1964, and while the stifling of antimilitary views was one factor, the general catalysts had to do with the actions of campus administrators and police. A useful summary of the rise of the FSM and its relationship to later student protests can be found in William O'Neill, *Coming Apart: An Informal History of America in the 1960s* (New York: Times Books, 1971), pp. 279–284.

22. "Berkeley Youth Leader Warns of Protests at Other Campuses," by Thomas Buckley, *New York Times*, December 12, 1964.

23. Clark Kerr, *The Uses of the University* (Cambridge, Massachusetts: Harvard University Press, 2001), p. 93. While Savio might not have read Kerr's book in full, he did later acknowledge that he had been influenced by a pamphlet circulated in October 1964 called "The Mind of Clark Kerr," which selectively quotes from Kerr's book to paint him as a quasi-fascist. See Savio's introduction to Hal Draper's *Berkeley: The New Student Revolt* (New York: Grove Press, 1965). See also Kerr's reference to the pamphlet and Savio in Kerr's memoir *The Gold and the Blue* (Berkeley: University of California Press, 2003), vol. 2, pp. 152–153.

24. These figures come from Kerr, *Uses of the University*, pp. 40–41.

25. An exhaustive roundup of how various universities treated allegedly radical professors is Lionel S. Lewis, *Cold War on Campus* (New Brunswick, New Jersey: Transaction Publishers, 1988). Most cases in the book involve potential violations against laws

prohibiting various aspects of the Communist Party, but it is clear that universities receiving public funds were especially wary about political dissidence among their faculty.

26. This oft-cited quote is sourced to an SDS pamphlet compiled by Carl Davidson, who cites a Hannah speech given at Parents' Convocation at Michigan State University, September, 1961. See Carl Davidson, *The New Radicals in the Multiversity* (Chicago: Charles H. Kerr Publishing, 1990), p. 11.

27. There are two useful books on the MSU experience in Vietnam. One was written by actual program participants: Robert Scigliano and Guy H. Fox, *Technical Assistance in Vietnam: The Michigan State University Experience* (New York: Frederick A. Praeger, 1965). The other is a well-researched historical overview: John Ernst, *Forging a Fateful Alliance: Michigan State University and Vietnam* (East Lansing: Michigan State University Press, 1998).

28. John A. Hannah, *A Memoir* (East Lansing: Michigan State University Press, 1980), p. 130.

29. Scigliano and Fox, *Technical Assistance*, p. 60.

30. Sidney Lens, *The Military-Industrial Complex* (Philadelphia: Pilgrim Press, 1970), p. 130.

31. Addendum to notes for the President, November 23, 1963. EL, DDE post-presidential papers, Augusta-Walter Reed Series, Box 2, Folder: Johnson, President Lyndon B., 1963.

32. Milton Eisenhower Oral History, September 1967, pp. 52 ff. Milton made similar remarks in his memoir *The President Is Calling* (New York: Doubleday, 1974), p. 363.

SEVEN

In Full Fury

1. A thoughtful, well-reported account of the Harvard incident and its aftermath is Robert J. Samuelson, "War on Campus: What Happened When Dow Visited Harvard," *Science*, New Series, vol. 158, no. 3806 (Dec. 8, 1967), pp. 1289–1294.

2. The "most abusive" quotation is from Don Whitehead, *The Dow Story: The History of the Dow Chemical Company* (New York:

McGraw-Hill, 1968), p. 262. The Dow memorandum is attributed to J. J. Boddie, and cited in David Maraniss, *They Marched Into Sunlight* (New York: Simon and Schuster, 2004), p. 71.

3. "Proxmire Charges Equipment Misuse," *New York Times*, December 27, 1967; "Proxmire Links 23 Contractors to Defense Waste," *New York Times*, January 6, 1968.

4. This phrase is the title of chapter 5 of William Proxmire, *Report from Wasteland: America's Military-Industrial Complex* (New York: Praeger Publishers, 1970).

5. Arnold Kanter, "Congress and the Defense Budget: 1960–1970," *The American Political Science Review*, vol. 66. No. 1 (March 1972), pp. 129–143. A pivotal work about Congress's role in military spending is Gordon Adams, *The Iron Triangle: The Politics of Defense Contracting* (New Brunswick, New Jersey: Transaction Books, 1982). Some of the most thorough recent research into the relationship between Congress and military procurement can be found in Barry S. Rundquist and Thomas M. Carsey, *Congress and Defense Spending* (University of Oklahoma Press, 2002). There are also several relevant essays in Alex Mintz, ed., *The Political Economy of Military Spending in the United States* (New York: Routledge, 1992). A case for the strong influence of public opinion on military spending can be found in "Public Opinion: A Powerful Predictor of U.S. Defense Spending," by Robert Higgs and Anthony Kilduff, in Higgs's fascinating book *Depression, War and Cold War* (New York: Oxford University Press, 2006), pp. 195–207.

6. Richard F. Kaufman, "As Eisenhower was saying . . . 'We Must Guard Against Unwarranted Influence By the Military-Industrial Complex,'" *New York Times Magazine*, June 22, 1969, p. 10.

7. Leonard S. Rodberg and Derek Shearer, eds., *The Pentagon Watchers: Students Report on the National Security State* (Garden City, New York: Doubleday, 1970), p. 2.

8. The Council on Economic Priorities, *Efficiency In Death: The Manufacturers of Anti-Personnel Weapons* (New York: Harper and Row, 1970).

9. Seymour Melman, *Disarmament: Its Politics and Economics* (Boston: American Academy of Arts and Sciences, 1962). See also

Melman's series with Praeger Publishers, including *Local Economic Development after Military Base Closures.*

10. Seymour Melman, *Our Depleted Society* (New York: Dell, 1965), p. 95.

11. Seymour Melman, *Pentagon Captialism* (New York: McGraw-Hill, 1970), p. 34.

12. Murray Weidenbaum, "Arms and the American Economy: A Domestic Convergence Hypothesis," *American Economic Review*, vol. 58, no. 2 (May 1968), pp. 428–437.

13. John Kenneth Galbraith, *The New Industrial State* (Boston: Houghton Mifflin, 1967), p. 393.

14. John Kenneth Galbraith, "The Big Defense Firms Are Really Public Firms and Should Be Nationalized," *New York Times Magazine*, November 16, 1969, pp. 50 ff.

15. See, for example, J. A. Stockfisch, *Plowshares Into Swords: Managing the American Defense Establishment* (New York: Mason and Lipscomb, 1973), pp. 271–272.

16. David A. Andelman, "Navy Buys $1.7-Million in Stock of Ailing Defense Plant on L.I.," *New York Times*, December 27, 1972.

17. "Contractors—The Navy as Banker," *TIME*, January 15, 1973.

18. "Soldiers and Scholars," *Phi Delta Kappan*, May 1967, p. 417.

19. An excellent account of how opinions about Pentagon-funded research shifted on two campuses can be found in Stuart W. Leslie, *The Cold War and American Science: The Military-Industrial-Academic Complex at MIT and Stanford* (New York: Columbia University Press, 1993).

20. See, for example, "Universities: The Case for Secret Research," *TIME*, November 21, 1967.

21. A richly detailed history of the CIA's involvement with the NSA and other cultural and political organizations can be found in Hugh Wilford's *The Mighty Wurlitzer: How the CIA Played America* (Cambridge, Massachusetts: Harvard University Press, 2008). The best one-volume guide to the treasure trove of FBI dirty tricks under COINTELPRO remains Ward Churchill and Jim Vander Wall, eds., *The COINTELPRO Papers* (Boston: South End Press, 1990).

22. J. W. Fulbright, *The Pentagon Propaganda Machine* (New York: Liveright Publishing, 1970), p. 142.
23. This account of Minnesota protests relies in part on Stanford E. Lehmberg and Ann M. Pflaum, *The University of Minnesota, 1945–2000* (Minneapolis: University of Minnesota Press, 2001), pp. 118–123. See also "War Foes Adopt Business Tactic," *New York Times*, December 28, 1969.

EIGHT
"Eisenhower Must Be Rolling Over in His Grave"

1. This was the title, for example, of a lengthy article by Eric Schlosser in *The Atlantic*, December 1998, pp. 51–77.
2. Barry Ritholtz with Aaron Task, *Bailout Nation: How Greed and Easy Money Corrupted Wall Street and Shook the World Economy* (Hoboken, New Jersey: John Wiley and Sons, 2009), p. 89.
3. Ismael Hossein-Zaden, *The Political Economy of U.S. Militarism* (New York: Palgrave Macmillan, 2006).
4. Robert Higgs, "The Cold War Economy: Opportunity Costs, Ideology, and the Politics of Crisis," chapter 6 of *Depression, War and Cold War* (Oakland, California: Independent Institute, 2006), pp. 124–151.
5. Leslie H. Gelb, "What Peace Dividend?" *New York Times*, Feb. 21, 1992.
6. I have benefited greatly from the work of Jurgen Brauer, professor of economics at Augusta State University. Brauer's extensive analysis of government spending figures includes several ways of measuring the concept of military spending, the definition of which inevitably involves political judgments. Charts showing the different methods of defining spending can be found at Brauer's website, http://www.aug.edu/~sbajmb/econdata_milex.pdf.
7. Alex Roland, *The Military-Industrial Complex* (Washington, D.C.: American Historical Association, 2001), p. 9.
8. These figures come from the Bureau of Economic Analysis, a division of the United States Commerce Department. The BEA fixes the value of the dollar to its worth in 2005, meaning that, given inflation, the dollars before 2005 are worth com-

paratively more and dollars after 2005 are worth comparatively less. By way of comparison, the "real" GDP in 2008 is $14.4 trillion, or some 26 times higher than the "real" 1961 GDP of $544.8 billion.

9. These figures are derived from a variety of government sources. I am relying on Jurgen Brauer's compilation of them (see note 6), using full military expenditures (which includes the budgets of the Defense Department and Veterans Affairs, plus military costs outside the Defense budget) as a percentage of per-capita GDP.

10. Walter Pincus, "Cargo Plane with Strings Attached," *Washington Post*, July 23, 1998. In subsequent years the Pentagon did begin requesting the construction of further C-130s.

11. See Barry S. Rundquist and Thomas M. Carsey, *Congress and Defense Spending: The Distributive Politics of Military Procurement* (Norman: University of Oklahoma Press, 2002), particularly chapters 5 and 9; and Bruce Russett, *What Price Vigilance?* (New Haven: Yale University Press, 1970).

12. Ann Markusen et al., *The Rise of the Gunbelt: The Military Remapping of Industrial America* (New York: Oxford University Press, 1991), pp. 12 ff. Curiously, Markusen's analysis of the MIC is one of the very few to downplay the role of Congress, arguing that it acts at best "as a protector and reinforcer of existing military economies rather than as a causal force" (p. 242).

13. Todd Sandler and Keith Hartley, *The Economics of Defense* (New York: Cambridge University Press, 1995), p. 220.

14. "The U.S. Employment Effects of Military and Domestic Spending Priorities: An Updated Analysis," Robert Pollin and Heidi Garrett-Peltier, Political Economy Research Institute (University of Massachusetts), October 2009.

15. Vernon W. Ruttan, *Is War Necessary for Economic Growth?* (New York: Oxford University Press, 2006), p. 162.

16. See, for example, Nance Goldstein, "Defense Spending as Industrial Policy: The Impact of Military R&D on U.S. Software Industry," in Gregory A. Bischak, ed., *Towards a Peace Economy in the United States* (New York: St. Martin's Press, 1991).

17. A number of recent books have discussed the abuses in Iraq in

the context of broader problems with the structure of today's military, including Jim Frederick, *Black Hearts: One Platoon's Descent Into Madness In Iraq's Triangle of Death* (New York: Random House, 2010) and Jeremy Scahill, *Blackwater: The Rise of the World's Most Powerful Mercenary Army* (New York: Nation Books, 2009). The issue of private contractors' influence on foreign policy is thoughtfully treated in Allison Stanger, *One Nation Under Contract: The Outsourcing of American Power and the Future of Foreign Policy* (New Haven: Yale University Press, 2009).

18. Aaron L. Friedberg, *In the Shadow of the Garrison State: America's Anti-Statism and Its Cold War Grand Strategy* (Princeton: Princeton University Press, 2000), p. 340.

19. A particularly harrowing account of the abuses of justice surrounding Guantanamo is Murat Kurnaz, *Five Years of My Life: An Innocent Man in Guantanamo* (New York: Palgrave Macmillan, 2008).

20. The figures and analysis of the Nixon administration's switch to private arms sales is taken from chapter 3 of John Tirman, *Spoils of War: The Human Cost of America's Arms Trade* (New York: The Free Press, 1997).

21. William Hartung, *And Weapons For All* (New York: Harper Collins, 1994). Thom Shanker, "Despite Slump, U.S. Role as Top Arms Supplier Grows," *New York Times*, September 7, 2009.

Index